# Income Double / Half the Trouble

Also by Jonathan Flaks

"Who Are You, Inc. – Bringing Out Your Best in Business"

(audio CD)

# INCOME DOUBLE /
# HALF THE TROUBLE

*Fundamentals and Breakthroughs for
Business and Personal Success*

**Jonathan Flaks**

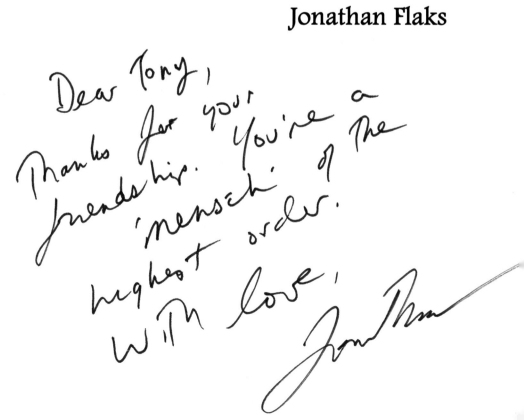

Dear Tony,
Thanks for your
friendship. You're a
'mensch' of the
highest order.
With love,
Jonathan

This edition published by
Dog Ear Publishing
4010 W. 86th Street, Ste H
Indianapolis, IN 46268

www.dogearpublishing.net

ISBN: 978-160844-083-2
This book is printed on acid-free paper.

Printed in the United States of America

*For my kids, Nathan and Ray,*
*and for you who will make the world*
*a better place for them to live in.*

# Contents

# Contents

# Acknowledgements

*"Lots of people want to ride with you in the limo, but what you want is someone who will take the bus with you when the limo breaks down."*
*- Oprah Winfrey, entrepreneur*

There is no way I was going to write this book without help. In fact, I was considering creating a different book called, *I Refuse To Write This Book*. I was going to rant from an armchair and have someone else figure out what I meant to say. Writing a book is hard, but with the encouragement, feedback, support and talent of the following people, it got done without tremendous hardship. I am deeply grateful.

To my wife, first and foremost, for always being by my side, even after 20 years.

To my kids, Nathan and Ray, for great joy and fun. I'm very proud of you boys.

To Sloane Miller, my book coach and first round editor, who made sure I wrote one chapter at a time, and then made sure I rewrote and found good examples whenever they were needed. Sloane cared as much or more than I did about making sure this book was completed to the highest standards possible. She was like having a business partner. Big thanks, Sloane!

To Carrie Cantor for outstanding editorial ideas, support and guidance, and to Ryan Ratliff for the terrific cover art and interior graphics – nice work!

To Stan Corwin, whose deep experience in publishing and outstanding feedback was extremely helpful and inspiring. You're the man, Stan!

# Acknowledgements

To all of my clients who have engaged in coaching and given me outstanding opportunities to learn and grow with you. Special thanks to those clients who have allowed me to share their success stories on these pages and over the internet.

To Robert Buck, Persephone Zill, Mark Satterfield, Debra Brown-Volkman, Harry Small, Madeleine Homan, and all my mentors and coaches for great feedback, support and encouragement.

To Alexander Petruska, who was much more than my childhood piano teacher, he was my first "coach" and taught me how to listen.

To my business networking and master-mind groups, including the Westchester Business Network (WBN), the Infinite Achievement Circle (IAC), my new "Brain Trust, the International Coach Federation, and the Business Council of the Make-A-Wish Foundation's Hudson Valley Chapter. You know who you are – do you know how precious you are to me?

To Lindsey Jergensen, Jane Berger, Pam Mitchell, ZoeAnn Murphy, Nancy Shire, Margot Metzger, Ross Green, Ellen Ginsberg, Meg Beach-Hacking and Kris Krauskopf for keeping the administrative and financial details of my coaching business running smoothly.

To my health team, Dr. Randy Stein and Dr. Robert Shire, for keeping me in tip top shape.

To my closest friends, particularly Jeff Richter, Rob Shire, David Simkins, and Dennis Ullman – and particularly to Captain Edd Schillay and the crew of the *Starship Enterprise* (our yacht racing team), for all the fun, support, and excitement. Boldly we go!

To the guys in the band. Rock on!

And last, but not least, to my terrific sisters and brothers-in-law, and my adventurous and inspiring Mom and Dad. With all my love.

# Introduction

*"I do not live to play, but I play in order that I may live, and return with greater zest to the labors of life."*

*- Plato*

This is the kind of freedom I want to make possible for you, no matter what is happening in the economy:

The sails are full, the clear blue sky is dusted with wisps of clouds, and the hull slices purposefully through the Hudson River. A steady breeze tickles my face and musses my hair.

It's Thursday, 11:30 A.M.

I'm not a professional yachtsman, so perhaps I should be at work on a Thursday, like everyone else. Not today – this may be one of the best sailing days this season, and that's just how I roll! This is the kind of freedom I enjoy, and *this is the kind of freedom I want to make possible for you.*

As a business and life coach, I help people realize their potential and find satisfaction, freedom, and power in their work lives, all of which lead to a balance of well-being and happiness in their personal lives. My clients are primarily entrepreneurial CEOs and business owners, consultants, and professionals. They often say they are working too hard and not having fun anymore. They typically have gotten by with some level of success, but are eager to earn more money more easily. Whether or not they have been doing well financially, they come to me when they are worried about repeating certain mistakes or getting stuck *busting their butts* for years and years while missing out on the joys of free time, family and having a great balanced life.

I help them see things that they otherwise are missing, including a very clear sense of direction and purpose, which is inspiring. I help them brainstorm new ideas and implement exciting, do-able strategies to achieve their goals. I've helped many people double their income with half the trouble, and many others to thrive no matter what the economic conditions have been. But one thing that we always agree on is that there is more to life than just raking in the dough. We use a broader definition of income:

**Income is everything that you truly want to "come in" to your life, including, but not limited to, money.**

The good news is that this book provides a multitude of tools, perspectives, and practical strategies that directly and indirectly result in bringing in more money—perhaps twice what you've been earning so far. Money is certainly a key measure by which we judge success and, of course, is necessary in our society for food, a place to live, a decent car and all our basic needs and wants. The better news is that there are also many other things that you can double with half the trouble, such as valuable experiences, education, fun times, love and friendship, and other rewards you value.

If your life or self-image is driven largely by how much money you make, and you've been wondering that there must be more to life, then my methods will give you an integrated approach to life. I start from the premise that passion for life, for work, for one's activities, are all connected and feed on each other; they are not separate compartments. This realization, and the ability to put it into practice, is part of the key to success. The techniques that you will learn here will help you appreciate your worth, expand your horizons, reduce energy-draining constraints, and free up you ability to provide greater value and service to mankind – all of which will impact your ability to build your wealth. You will also be excited and motivated to get out of bed and engage in your business life every day. And you'll also be able to *enjoy* more time with your family and friends. Play more golf or tennis, learn to sail, join a band, paint, ride horses, go cross-country on a Harley or whatever your dream is. When you go on vacation, you'll be on a REAL vacation with the cell phone OFF! It is a holistic approach.

Which of the following statements do you relate to the most?

- "I'd really like to get out of this rut and wake up excited for work every day."

- "I'm fed up with my career, but I'm not sure how to take the next steps."
- "I've got to stop spinning my wheels and flitting from task to task."
- "I'm not running my business – it's running me!"
- "I need a better process for making contacts and building my professional network."
- "My family and I are sick and tired of how busy and consumed I am beyond work hours."
- "It's time for me to start earning what I am truly worth."
- "There has got to be a better way!"

After 20 years in business consulting and 10 years running a coaching company, these are the kinds of concerns I hear from people most often. These concerns show both restlessness and a readiness to take one's life/work to the next level of excellence. If that kind of anxiousness has attracted you to this book, then you're in for a brighter future. By changing the way you look at, think about, and make decisions in your personal and business life, you will live with confidence, passion, joy, and strength.

My method is fairly simple—it is a three-phase process—but getting through it involves commitment, positive thinking, self-discipline, and ability to follow through. It doesn't replace one-on-one coaching if you really want to be on the fast track to a success that fits you like a glove, and it doesn't replace therapy if you're in serious trouble.

This book is *not* a "get rich quick" scheme, "millionaire mind game" or a manual for investing in real estate or the stock market. You'll soon see some basic math, evidence and examples that this is about a realistic, attainable goal.

It's a home-coaching course, perhaps the first and only home-coaching program you've had in book form. Unlike most books, CD's and home-study programs filled with content about a subject, this home-coaching program is a framework and series of thought provoking tools that provide perspective on the content of *your* life. When you've finished this book, you'll see that it's actually a book about you – the new you!

If it's time to be as extraordinary as you can be, read on!

## HOW "INCOME DOUBLE / HALF THE TROUBLE" WAS BORN

I started coaching in 1998, after 12 years of diverse business communication experience. Along the way, I had always been approached and been helpful to people seeking career, business and interpersonal advice, so it was natural for me to move into the relatively new coaching industry. I found out soon after that I was one of the first and fastest to build up a successful coaching practice.

A few years later, I read an article about a mortgage broker who increased her income by 200% in one year. That impressive result piqued my interest in coaching my clients to get that kind of return.

Blair, a client who had a comfortable consulting income, was hungry to earn more money but also wanted spend more quality time with his wife and newborn daughter. I believed that he was the kind of person who would probably go for a big challenge, like the person I read about in the magazine article who doubled her income. I figured he would, at the very least, appreciate the invitation, even if he decided not to accept my challenge.

So I asked him, "How would you like to actively focus on doubling your income with half the trouble?" I suggested that if we aimed for this new target, we would certainly have an exciting series of conversations and discoveries, regardless of the outcome. After a short discussion, he said, "Okay!" and we went right to work.

First, we had to get real about the goal: Was it attainable? Next, we had to clean out any negative thinking that was holding him back in old habits and eliminate distractions. As a creative person, Blair had a lot of enthusiasm, and was often scattered in many directions. Then, we reorganized his priorities to identify his best bets. By focusing primarily on choices that would bring the greatest return for his time and energy, he leveraged the heck out of the resources he already had at his fingertips or that were within reasonable reach.

Over the next six months, Blair's business grew dramatically. Online sales for one of his side projects, the Pile Cabinet, increased from $1,000 per month to $8,000 per month; during a peak month shortly thereafter, he posted $13,000 in revenue. This software product required very little increase in expenses as his online revenue expanded, so virtually all of this growth passed through directly as personal income. It continues to be an income generator for Blair that requires only a few hours a week of attention.

Blair also applied the concepts we discussed to a nonprofit drum and dance center, his other passion. Without increasing his part-time schedule, he led the organization to grow in size, capacity, stature, and financial health. In 2006, Bush-Mango Drum and Dance Center earned the greater Rochester area's Cultural Organization of the Year award, and Blair was able to double his and his partner's salaries.

Upon celebrating the financial victory, Blair also told me, "I've crushed the notion that I can't make money as a musician!" His joy from this revelation is the most exciting outcome for me. Blair is an example of someone who increased his "income" both in terms of monetary earnings and sense of satisfaction with the way he spends his time and what he offers to his community.

The experience of working with Blair showed me that sometimes a tremendous amount of one's potential is held back for fairly simple reasons, and I found I had a knack for identifying those issues and helping people overcome them.

When I discovered that I had found ways that work, I decided to share it with more and more people. I used these techniques with more individual coaching clients and soon thereafter created a group coaching program, called "Income Double / Half the Trouble." I got outstanding testimonials from clients who experienced significant returns in the program (see what they have to say at www.incomedouble.info).

Given the constraints on my time for individual and group coaching programs, I made it my business to capture that material into the home-coaching program you now have in your hands. I wanted to make sure the concepts and frameworks that have worked so well for so many people do not end up stuck in my head. They belong out in the open, with you.

## It's Lonely at the Top

Entrepreneurs and self-employed professionals have the most potential for the benefits and breakthroughs that this coaching program offers, although employees with entrepreneurial minds can gain a lot as well I have found that most of the entrepreneurs, consultants, and professionals I've met, even if they have partners and/or staff, can sometimes feel a bit lonely and isolated. Many studies show that the self-employed work more hours than those with salaried jobs, are more likely to work on weekends, and are less likely to take time off for illness. However, they demonstrate higher levels of job satisfaction, higher levels of "self-efficacy" (a person's belief about his or her ability to accomplish a task or deal with the challenges of life), and lower levels of depression than salaried workers.

I admire entrepreneurs and the self-employed because you have a fire in the belly and can get excited about the possibilities, risks and challenges you face – even the hardest struggles can become opportunities with the right frame of mind. In times of trouble, with frightening obstacles in the way, if you can *truly believe* in a greater possibility—creative energy comes rushing through. Fear and apathy dissolve and things really start to happen. Time and time again, my clients generate and act on new ideas and attract new resources and sources of income. Sometimes solutions arise from out of nowhere to support their courageous goals. Things just start gelling, and it's an amazing experience.

I try to nurture this spirit among employed people as well as those who own or manage professional service firms. If you can get in touch with this spirit within yourself and be true to it, you will succeed in accomplishing whatever goals you had in mind when you picked up this book.

## DEFINITIONS

There are a few important terms we need to define and emphasize for the purposes of this book. These are words that refer to crucial elements to the process of expanding possibilities for growth and success. They are: *assets, beliefs, commitment, income, leverage,* and *trouble.* Even just understanding these words in a new way and making them part of your vocabulary can be a first step towards expanding your horizons. I recommend that you bookmark this page and refer back to it from time to time as you go through the exercises in this book.

**Assets:** Your assets include all of your resources, including material objects, ideas, thoughts, beliefs, and relationships, within reach that can or do *generate* income and/or can be leveraged to generate *multiple levels* of income.

**Beliefs:** Your beliefs are habits of thought about so-called truths that drive your behavior. Beliefs can be changed. We can "frame-shift" and change our beliefs and attitudes, leading to new behavior, a personality that attracts people and opportunities, and better results. In Part 1, you will focus on identifying your negative beliefs and learn how to replace them with honest, positive beliefs that will help you naturally attract what you want in life.

**Commitment:** Your commitment is your willingness to pursue an outcome and do what it takes to make it work; to bring a joyful, excited, faithful, hopeful, and confident energy to a pursuit that is challenging and to play to win. If you are committed to something, you take unsuccessful attempts and consider them instructive steps toward the greater commitment rather than consider them failures.

**Income:** Your income is whatever you want to "come in" to your life. It is not limited to money. Most of us value time with friends and family, travel, education, creative freedom, etc. This broader definition of income, and how to increase it, is an important part of what this book is all about.

**Leverage (v.):** You leverage your assets by multiplying the positive income productivity of any asset you have in your life. In Part 3, we explore how to leverage resources as the means to "duplicate" your income.

**Trouble:** Trouble is anything that interferes with income or enjoyment of life. It can be internal beliefs or external obstacles or both. In Part 2, we focus on deleting your troubles, with the goal of cutting them in half.

## The 80/20 Rule Illustrated

Another important concept we will discuss in this book is Pareto's Principle, one that is commonly known in the business world as the 80/20 rule. According to many studies, 80% of results come from

20% of efforts. For example, in sales organizations, 80% of revenues consistently come from 20% of the sales force. Many corporate reorganizations involve identifying that crucial 20% and eliminating less productive assets and liabilities.

If you relate this principle to your own life and business career, you can mathematically prove the realistic, attainable nature of having your income double. Consider what would happen if you could identify the 20% of your actions, resources, and relationships that generate 80% of your results and then focused only on those kinds of activities, increasing them by one and a half times. You would then use only 50% of your energy and time (20+20+10= 50%), but would thereby duplicate the matching result by one and a half times also, thereby producing twice the results (80+80+40 = 200% return!). Take a look at the graphic below (Figure 1) for further clarification of this mathematical model.

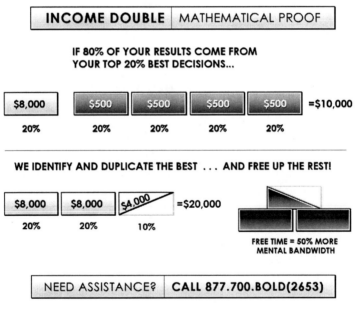

**Figure 1.** The 80-20 Rule illustrated. *Voila! If your goal is to have your income double with half the trouble, you eliminate the most wasteful blocks and focus on the most fruitful areas of your life that are worth leveraging.*

## THE THREE STEPS

The process we undertake is organized in three steps, and the book is divided accordingly into three parts. They are:

- Believe
- Delete
- Duplicate

The Believe step involves finding out what is in your head that might be holding you back or giving you unrealistic notions. The Delete step involves eliminating obstacles of all kinds. The Duplicate step involves doing *twice* as much of whatever produces your *best bets*. Let's look at each of the three a little more closely.

### Believe: Choosing Empowering Beliefs

The first step to having your income double with half the trouble is to believe in the possibility that it *can* be done without changing who you are. In fact, the more true you are to your core values, the easier it becomes. You don't have to change careers or suddenly become an expert in real estate, for example, if you don't want to—there is a way to harness your own true passions, talents and values (although you may have to change your approach a bit). You can live the life of your dreams and have more money or anything you want to "come in" to your life. You have the ability to choose empowering beliefs, and these will be the key to your success.

Part I instructs you on how to expand your belief systems. By understanding and eliminating the limiting beliefs that hold you back and replacing them with perspectives that empower you, you can access an infinite supply of passion, creativity, resourcefulness, and desire to set and achieve outstanding goals. This process is the foundation of this book. It is important to believe in the possibility of that goal if you are going to pursue it!

In order to be most successful, you will need to back your belief with commitment. The most important thing to believe is that there is no such thing as failure. After any unsuccessful efforts that fall short of reaching a specific, desire result, people either embrace the learning experience and keep going, or they quit trying. Quitting is what people usually equate with failure. But if you don't ever quit, you can't fail. You never have to consider any commitment a failure as long as you learn and grow from your experience and stay committed!

## Delete: Eliminate Drains on Your Time and Energy

Part 2 will walk you through the process of clearing the way for you to attract and seize on new opportunities in your life. You will remove the obstacles to efficient earning; some that you may not even have realized were getting in the way. By eliminating energy drains, trashing time-wasters, delegating mediocre involvements, and making changes as to whom you deal with and how you deal with them, you will have more time, energy, and *room* for everything that you truly want to have "come in" to your life. Sound hard? Not if you believe that it doesn't have to be done all at once. Every incremental improvement you make will provide a great sense of accomplishment and feelings of eagerness for the results that are destined to follow.

## Duplicate: Identify and "Leverage" the Diamonds in Your Gemfield

The third section of this book will guide you in identifying the very best of the resources and relationships within your reach so you can duplicate the aspects of your life that already bring you 80% of your income, both financial and otherwise. Only the most ideal resources, ideas, and relationships in your life will lead to the most ideal outcomes. It may seem easy to say no to situations that are clearly bad—although many people do accept far-less-than-ideal situations for various reasons. But it takes real courage, wisdom, and a lot of practice to say no to opportunities that are pretty good in order to free up time and energy for opportunities that are truly great. Saying "no" to what's *good* so you can focus only on what is *great* may seem simple in concept, but it is harder in practice.

— Let me tell you the story of a successful client as an example of how the whole process weaves together. We'll call him "Jeff" (but I respectfully keep his real name confidential). Jeff came to me at a point when he was already a leader, a top 15% producer in the executive recruiting industry. But he wanted to be a million-dollar-per-year producer. He wanted his income to double with half the trouble. He followed the three steps. First he believed. He often repeated the mantra, "I'm a million-dollar producer," and he committed to the goal by means of agreeing to follow my program. Meanwhile, he worked Part Two, which was to delete: He cleared out six file boxes of resumes and retained the one box of contact information that represented his most promising professionals. He also set up a system of communicating with potential candidates via email. It was a system he had previously not been successful or comfortable with, but by being bold and getting some help from his assistant, he was able to improve and implement the "distribution" method of updating potential candidates. In this way, he duplicated and actually quadrupled his ability to contact his best candidates.

Jeff made these adjustments, and over the course of six months, he doubled his income. He reported that he also has had more time for personal relationships, primarily with his wife, and was able to fix up and enjoy his summer home more often. You may think that this seems unrealistically simple—most breakthroughs are—but once he was actually organized and focused on his best bets, the rest came easily.

## THE CHALLENGE AHEAD

My challenge in this book is to try to distill the very best methods and concepts that lead to the successes of Blair, Jeff, and others who have succeeded at this level, so that I can help you without necessarily having one-on-one sessions in real time with you. I'm cramming a year's worth of coaching into a relatively small book! Of course, I recommend that you work with a real live coach. It is hard to describe how valuable that one-on-one interaction can be. But I have designed this book as a personalized home-coaching program that you can use either as part of a guided coaching program or simply by itself as a self-coaching tool. In the latter case, you are your own coach. The tools, techniques, models, and resources presented here are ones that have worked for many of my clients and can help you have twice the good stuff that you want to "come in" to your life while eliminating half of whatever gets in the way.

How exactly can *you* accomplish this leveraging feat and apply it to *your* own business, to *your* own life? That's the big question for you to ponder and consider as you progress through this book. There is no simple answer. You will have to find the specific ways yourself, by opening up your creative mental channels, by finding good advisors, by brainstorming with smart people you know, and other tactics. A business-savvy coach or marketing expert who gets to know a good deal about you and your particular business can help you come up with practical ideas, specific goals, and a step-by-step plan. But YOU must lead the process, whatever resources you use, to harness your energy and manage your time and your choices to create the greatest possible "income."

Having your income double with half the trouble doesn't happen overnight. The key to your success and experience with this book and this method is your active role in the process. Like a workbook, this book is full of suggestions, tools and charts, as well as thought-provoking questions and calls to action. You must fill in the blanks and do the homework in order to apply what you learn to your own situation. Be prepared with pen and paper, laptop, computer or BlackBerry, or whatever note taking and action planning tools work best for you. You may find yourself investing a week, a few weeks or even a full month per chapter to read, digest, understand, and, most importantly, apply the concepts and exercises in each chapter. You'll have lots of ideas and will want to prioritize and choose how you implement them. This is YOUR program, so YOU set your own pace and I invite you to **go for it** with your highest level of energy and commitment! Don't hesistate to contact me if you need guidance around anything or anyone that gets in the way of your success.

Take a few minutes now to look over the Table of Contents again so you have a sense of what lies ahead. Consider it a map for your upcoming adventure. You'll be more successful in facing some of the challenges that may arise if they are less of a surprise to you. And soon you will find doubling your income can be an attainable goal!

Now, let the adventure begin!

# Part I

## Believe

# Chapter 1

# The Foundations for Success

*"Most people search high and wide for the keys to success. If
they only knew, the key to their dreams lies within."*
*-George Washington Carver, botanist and scientist*

If you've ever painted an interior room in a home, or if you've seen
professionals do it, you know that a lot of time goes into preparation.
It takes time to move the furniture, cover the floors, and put masking
tape around the windows, light switches, and anything else that isn't
supposed to be painted. If patience and care are applied during preparation, the quality and speed of the job improves dramatically, as well
as the clean-up afterwards, compared to what would happen otherwise. The same is true for the bold goal of having your income double
with half the trouble. A lot of mental preparation is necessary for the
journey. It has to do with your own limiting beliefs about yourself and
what you can or cannot handle. In my experience coaching all kinds
of intelligent, talented, and motivated people, I have found again and
again that the biggest stumbling block to success is one's own mental
restrictions.

Here is an exercise that will show you how powerful beliefs can
be.

How many push-ups or sit-ups do you believe you can do in 30
seconds? Take a guess and write down a number here: _____

Okay, now go for it! That's right. Put the book down for 30 seconds and count how many push-ups or sit-ups you can do in that time.
Write down the number here: _____

Now, think of a really strong *reason* and desire to double the
number of push-ups or sit-ups you can do. Meanwhile, allow yourself

to entertain the belief that it is possible to double the number of repetitions you can achieve. How would you feel if you did accomplish that goal? Are you willing to set your mind, body, and soul to believing it is possible and go for it? When you are ready, put the book down and do another set, and then compare the number of push-ups or sit-ups to your previous trial.

Write it down here: _____

Did the number go up? Did it double? Why or why not?

_____

_____

_____

_____

_____

Whenever I do this experiment at leadership training sessions, the numbers almost ALWAYS go up. Sometimes they double and, in a few cases, even triple when people have a compelling, motivating reason *why* they wanted to do more push-ups or sit-ups! In one case, a participant who felt a cold coming on chose to believe that by doing more sit-ups she would strengthen her whole immune system. She tripled the number of sit-ups she was able to do, even though she was feeling tired and weak. How did your results relate to your thoughts, desire, purpose, and beliefs about doing push-ups?

The key to having your income double with half the trouble is orienting your belief system around the possibility and purpose of reaching your goal. It is mission critical to believe in compelling, heartfelt reasons that it can happen to you and can be done without changing who you are. In fact, the more authentic you are to your core values, the easier it becomes.

Try saying this out loud, and see how it feels to you:

**"I am going to double my income with half the trouble over the course of the next year."** Do you feel it stirring and inspiring as a believable possibility, or are you still carrying around a perfectly normal and healthy amount of doubt? Whatever your level of belief right now, it is fairly certain that you have already begun to believe it *is* truly possible. Why do I think that? Because you are reading this book! Would you have decided to read a book entitled *Income Double / Half the Trouble* if you couldn't believe it were possible and even likely? Would you buy a book called *How to Play for a Professional NBA Team* if you didn't believe in your abilities as a basketball player? Would you invest time and money on *How to Be a World-Class Rock Star* if you didn't believe in your musical talent?

So kudos to you for already beginning to believe in your own potential for doubling your income with half the trouble. Even though I know from my experience with many people that it *is* possible and realistic, I know it takes a certain degree of courage and confidence for you to believe in such a goal. Kudos to you!

Now let's take that energy to the next level.

Imagine it is one year from today. Close your eyes and envision your success. See yourself surrounded by the things you desire and the people (or kind of people) you love most. Imagine with all your senses that you are experiencing a life of your ideal design. Imagine you can smell the fine foods from your kitchen or favorite restaurant. Taste the pina colada served to you at the tropical beach where you spend half your time. Listen to the music–go to every concert! Feel how good it feels to be balanced, healthy, wealthy, and happy. Now, imagine that you can capture this image and the feelings and put it into a glass marble that you can put in your pocket and revisit anytime you want. (Perhaps you will be well served to find a talisman—a small, tangible object that represents and reminds you of this feeling in an instant.) If you start *today* enjoying the experience of your ideal success, even if imaginary at this point, you can immediately begin to enjoy your success within the *feeling* of being successful.

Perhaps there are goals you aren't pursuing now because you don't believe they are possible. You probably have some really good reasons you could cite as to why they are not possible for you. But what if, instead, you were to consider yourself infinitely creative and resourceful and therefore could believe in new possibilities? What ways to get closer to your goals would you uncover and pursue? Win or lose, wouldn't you learn a lot about your potential along the way?

Go ahead and write down a few goals that you would pursue if you felt they were realistic.

_____

_____

_____

_____

_____

_____

Just bringing these thoughts to the surface is a big step. All your actions are driven by your beliefs. Getting started with the right foundation is mission critical.

The intention and purpose of this first section is to prepare you for the range of emotions that you will likely encounter as you move forward. Your preparation will help you gather up the necessary courage and preserve your energy and commitment for the road ahead.

---

### Challenge Homework:

1. Practice imagining with all your senses your ideal success every day, and journal or create a collage of your dream for an ideal future.
2. Write down a few goals and challenges that would be integral to your success, and begin to consider and write down what beliefs either support or conflict with your pursuit of these goals.

---

# Chapter 2
# Identifying Limiting Beliefs

*"If you want to be successful, it's just this simple: Know what you're doing. Love what you're doing. And believe in what you're doing."*

*- Will Rogers*

What is your energy like when you believe your current pursuit may be destined for mediocrity or failure?

How is your energy different when you need to get something done and you know you can do it well and it is likely to yield great results?

How do your beliefs affect your energy and your results? Beliefs have been proven to be a significant ingredient in confidence, learning, and growth. For example, one recent study showed that college students who believe intelligence is "a fixed entity" tend to emphasize "performance goals," leaving them overly influenced by negative feedback and likely to avoid challenging learning opportunities. In contrast, students who believe intelligence is "malleable" tend to emphasize "learning goals" and "rebound better from occasional failures."[1]

Our beliefs must be strong and aligned to what we desire, or we won't put in the energy to follow up with persistence to go after what

---

[1] Students who believe that feedback can enhance their malleable intelligence were able to correct 10 percent more errors when retested than students who perceive feedback as criticism of their limited intelligence. From Mangels JA, Butterfield B, Lamb J, Good C, Dweck C. 2006. Why do beliefs about intelligence influence learning success? A social cognitive neuroscience model. *Soc Cogn Affect Neurosci* 1(2):75-86.

we want to achieve. All of our actions and everything we create in our external environment is tied to our system of beliefs. The most successful people I know have positive, clear belief systems about their capacity for wealth. What I have discovered often as a coach is that people who are not achieving the kind of success they want are actually holding themselves back because of negative, unproductive, limiting beliefs about what they are capable of, what is appropriate for them socially, and what they deserve or are worthy of. These beliefs are often inaccurate, and people can be completely unaware that such beliefs hold them back. The first step in enhancing your success is to identify your beliefs about yourself: your strengths and talents, your value, your social role, and your feelings about success — particularly monetary success.

## PERSONAL INCOME CEILING

Let's begin exploring the belief system that defines your *Personal Income Ceiling*.

A five-gallon jug cannot hold more than five gallons of water. Similarly, your income will never exceed the Personal Income Ceiling that is programmed into your belief system. So let's break through that system, first by identifying the factors that make it up, and then by challenging and replacing the beliefs that limit your Personal Income Ceiling through a frame-shifting process.

Three elements make up your Personal Income Ceiling Belief System:

**Ability** – What you believe you can or cannot *handle*.

**Social Influences** – Beliefs about what is appropriate or what would bring about consequences in your relationships, family, work groups, and other communities. These notions can limit what you feel you are *allowed* to say, ask, or do.

**Self-Worth** – An inner sense of what you believe you truly *deserve*.

Beliefs are not only about what we *think* is true; they are deeper. They are tied to internalized experiences and emotions that we are sometimes unaware of. Some beliefs are obvious to you, and you are consciously aware of them. For example, you know that there are four seasons every year, and you know that you don't believe in a groundhog that determines when the winter season comes to an end. You know that you don't trust_____ to borrow your car and return it in the same condition (fill in the blank about someone who obviously fits that description.)

Other beliefs are hidden but can be brought to light. Have you ever procrastinated about confronting someone who you otherwise thought you could talk to about anything? If so, your belief that such a confrontation would be risky or unbearably uncomfortable is contrary to your perception of the openness in the relationship. For the length of time you procrastinated, your beliefs were running your behavior in the matter.

Your beliefs about money, income, success, and happiness are interwoven in a system that has brought you to where you are today. Think about the three words *rich, successful,* and *wealthy,* and jot down some impressions that come to mind.

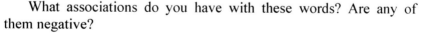

What associations do you have with these words? Are any of them negative?

When you have an awareness and power over the limiting beliefs that get in the way of your success, you will be free to create unlimited wealth, happiness, and balance.

Let's explore the three elements that typically affect personal income ceiling beliefs and then work on shifting those beliefs.

## Ability

Did you know that along with some accurate knowledge of what you are capable of, you also carry many inaccurate beliefs about what you are truly capable of *doing* or *handling* to create a super successful life? How many times have you held back actions or communications because you believed you wouldn't be able to handle the process or even the outcome?

Think about how often you've had any of the following thoughts:

- If I present myself as an expert and get tripped up on a question, people will think that I'm a fraud.
- I'm good at what I do, but I don't know how to sell myself.
- I can do A, B, and C really well, but because I'm weak on D, I'm just not good enough.
- I'm not a people person; my sister/brother was always the people person in the family.
- I'd like to expand into that new territory, but the learning curve is too big.

The idea here is to identify the not-so-apparent beliefs about your own abilities that might be hindering you. In most cases, just being aware of them can help you pull out from under their repressive effects. In some cases, examining them will show you that they are simply not accurate or not relevant, and that realization can free up your energy. Look at the chart below and fill in the blanks at the bottom with examples from your own life.

| Examples of things people DO because they believe they CAN: | Examples of things people DON'T do because they believe they CAN'T: |
| --- | --- |
| Tie shoes | Tie complex knots on sailboats |
| Make CERTAIN phone calls | Make OTHER phone calls |
| Make change of $20 | Make the right investments in securities |
| Drive a car | Fix a car |
| Pay bills | Calculate payroll taxes |
| Buy things on the Internet | Set up an e-commerce website |

| Something you do because you are really good at it: | Something you don't do because you believe you're not good enough: |
| --- | --- |
| _____ <br><br> _____ | _____ <br><br> _____ |

When you don't believe you have the ability to complete a task or handle the success or failure of a goal, do you find yourself avoiding or procrastinating on that task? Is it a fear of failure? Is it a fear of what you might be responsible for if you succeed? Either way, your concern about your *ability* to handle the challenges you may face can interfere with your motivation to move forward. In this way, beliefs about ability make up an important component of your capacity for income.

Instead, reframe your beliefs and consider the possibility that you are infinitely creative and resourceful – you can learn to do almost anything, or you can find the right people to do things for you! I have based my life's work on the premise that although there might be some blocks or obstacles I have to help people navigate, they are infinitely creative and resourceful – and when I share that philosophy with clients, they are usually able to overcome all hurdles and accomplish amazing results. You'll be seeing more stories that prove that point as you continue to read this book. But for now, just ponder the concept thought and let it sink in. Let yourself connect with your own true experiences to confirm this thought and make it a belief that can inspire you. We'll do more on reframing your beliefs in the next chapter.

## Social Influences

We also have limiting beliefs about our place in society or in relationships. We believe there are limits to what we're allowed to do or what is appropriate. This includes a healthy perspective on what is punishable by law or frowned upon according to social mores or norms. But there are also times when we think an action or communication is inappropriate or "that's not the way it's done around here," when in fact, there **are** ways to move forward boldly yet appropriately.

Within organizations or companies, very often people limit their communication, their sharing of information, and their collaborative efforts because of their feeling that there are unspoken rules about what is allowed or appropriate. Such perceptions about unspoken rules might include the following:

- I shouldn't speak directly to clients without the account executive's permission, or it will seem like I'm stepping on his toes.
- If I say what I really think, people will consider me too ambitious and won't like me.
- I'm just an ordinary person, but I better come up with a big, competitive idea to stay afloat in this big, competitive world.
- If I give my honest opinion about how so-and-so is failing, he/she will consider it an insult and I'll get a reputation for being negative.

As a result, honesty and constructive criticism are limited. This kills companies' potential.

| Things people DO because it seems allowed or appropriate | Things people DON'T DO because they seem disallowed or inappropriate |
|---|---|
| Say please and thank you<br>Interrupt someone reading email<br>Order pizza for delivery<br>Talk about the weather forecast<br>Call someone for a first date or meeting<br>Use foul language among friends<br>Send someone flowers on their birthday<br>Invite someone over to your house | Ask a superior to say please and thank you<br>Interrupt someone on the telephone<br>Order take-out from a 5-star restaurant<br>Talk about how someone might get fired<br>Call someone every day and don't give up<br>Use foul language in an art museum<br>Send someone flowers for no reason<br>Invite yourself over to someone else's house |

Small-business owners face challenges from limiting social beliefs as well. Often these beliefs limit their ideas about how successful they feel they are allowed to become. Some examples:

- One shouldn't boast or toot one's own horn.
- If I become too successful, my friends and family will think that I've "sold out."
- Clients/customers won't work with me unless I give them a severely reduced rate.
- If I ask too many questions about clients' needs and budgets, they will think I'm a shark, only in it for the money.

Do any of these statements apply to you or remind you of your own limiting beliefs? If so, which ones? What are the specifics of your situation? Write them down. If none of these statements apply to you but have got you thinking about some limiting beliefs you do have regarding your abilities, write them down here:

_____

_____

_____

This is a new day. Once you work through your limiting beliefs, you will no longer be limited by what *seems* appropriate to say or ask. The time has come to *find* the appropriate way to say or ask *anything* you have to say or ask. What have you been holding back that you could approach differently, and how else could you go about it?

_____

_____

_____

## Self-Worth

Our sense of worthiness is hard to get a grip on, as it operates invisibly in the depths of our minds and hearts. I see the self-worth factor as being like the alternator in a car. As most of us know, a car has a battery and an engine, but it also has this little thing called an alternator connecting the two. We don't see it, we don't hear much about it (hopefully!), and many of us don't even know what it is, but it's there, playing an essential role: It recharges the battery while the car is driving so that the car will start up again the next time we need it.

Your self-worth factor may be harder to visualize than an alternator in a car, but it is the most important of the beliefs in this system. If you look at the amount of money you have, the amount of money you make, how hard you work, and all the basic elements of your life, you have a picture of exactly what you believe you deserve. Your current life is filled with exactly what you have been willing to allow into your life and what you've allowed yourself to put up with. This element is tied to your emotional sense of *self-worth,* which is deeper than what you *think* or *say* you deserve.

See if any of the following statements make you squirm at little – for best results, say each one out loud and see how you feel:

- I'm pretty good at what I do, but I'm nothing compared to _____ (the foremost expert in this field).
- My father made me feel I would never amount to much, and I'm always trying to figure out if he was right.
- I'm not sure I provide a service that's worth all that much, when you really think about it.
- Aughh – how could I have made such a mistake? Now I understand why I am not appreciated!
- I tend to allow a few small failures to define me more than my many successes.

All too often, people wonder if they are valued and on the right path when a recent interaction goes sour – apparently forgetful of all the positive interactions that preceded it.

Have you noticed that there is a gap between what is fair compensation in the marketplace and how much you are comfortable asking for at any given time? If you discount your price too often and then feel underpaid, you are dealing with a discounted worthiness factor. If you overprice yourself, you may also be suffering from a misaligned sense of self-worth that you are trying to compensate for.

However, if you upgrade your worthiness factor beliefs, your sense of self-worth becomes limitless, and therefore you will be more naturally inclined to find ways to leverage your ability and talent to provide greater value. And you'll also be more open to earning more money—joyfully, courageously, creatively, and with greater ease.

Write down any limiting beliefs you think you might have that relate to self-worth:

_____

_____

_____

Now that you've started understanding your limiting beliefs, you can start to get them out of your way, through a process called frame-shifting.

# Chapter 3

# Frame-Shifting

*"If you don't like something, change it - if you can't change it, change your attitude."*
*Maya Angelou, author*

Limiting beliefs are *habits* — some can be as easy to change as learning to back up your computer every day. Other belief habits can be as difficult to change as quitting smoking or staying on a diet. Scientific models show that our brains have a tendency to program behavior into automatic habits whenever possible.

The good news is...*we* are the programmers! *We* are the designers of those brain patterns, and *we* can alter our habits and thoughts. Think of how often you have changed your mind, like deciding you were going to go to a party, then deciding to stay home. Have you ever avoided making a tough phone call and then found encouragement to go for it? Some thoughts can change direction like a summer breeze. Others may take an entire season to change. Let's look at techniques to shift and expand beliefs—a key to growth. Although it may be uncomfortable at times, it is very worthwhile to expand beyond your current limiting beliefs.

The experience of an actor I coached is a fascinating case study in how limiting beliefs can be identified and then changed, with the result being a whole new lease on life. A financially struggling (yet award-winning) actor for most of his adult life, this forty-five-year-old man hired me to help him find a new direction for his work in theater. In the course of our conversations, we were able to uncover some entrenched beliefs he held about his identity as a "struggling artist" that were getting in the way of putting forth the energy needed to break out of the rut he was in. He came to realize that he had become so wrapped up in being a "frustrated, angry, suffering actor" that he was overlooking the fact that his vast experience on the stage had endowed him with a tremendously valuable breadth of experience, insight, and empathy. He realized that he had the skills, experience, and desire to become a director, and even some of the connections to make it happen. But he realized that the first and most crucial step was to identify and then debunk his limiting beliefs.

He described the experience as being like when a barber shows you the back of your head by putting a mirror behind you. For a split second, you're not sure where to look. Then you make the shift to looking in the mirror in front of you to see the mirror behind you, and you suddenly see yourself from an entirely different perspective—from outside yourself. Once he made the frame shift, he was able to step-by-step do what he needed to do to turn his career around. He went on to become a working director and landed seven excellent shows in a row – he never had to "play the role" of the suffering actor again.

Let's put frame-shifting directly into practice. Think of a particular challenge or untapped opportunity, some recent or current goal that you want to achieve but have either avoided pursuing or tried but are unable to get past some block along the way. Ultimately, the purpose of frame-shifting is to zero in on beliefs that disempower you and replace them with those that empower you. Perhaps you can look back at your notes from the previous chapter for your own examples.

We will not deny your disempowering beliefs – instead we will focus on *other truths* that are at least as powerful—and a lot more useful to believe.

I suggest you make a few copies of the tool on the next page and be ready to fill in the boxes as we go through this tutorial. If your handwriting is too large for the boxes, make an enlarged photocopy of the tool or go to www.jf-executive-coaching.com/frame.xls and print as many copies as you need. Each time you work with this tool, you will expand your limiting beliefs. As you become more empowered through practice, watch for outcomes that you used to consider extremely unlikely.

INSTRUCTIONS:

## FRAME-SHIFTING FRAME

FOR EACH OF YOUR TOP 3-5 LIMITING BELIEFS, USE A SEPARATE COPY OF THIS ONE-PAGE TOOL.
THINK HARD AND DIG DEEP TO GET THE MOST VALUE. IF YOU GET STUCK, WORK WITH A COACH TO COMPLETE THE
ENTIRE EXERCISE. PRACTICE OPERATING WITH YOUR NEW BELIEF AND TAKE WRITTEN NOTES TO TRACK THE BENEFITS
YOU EXPERIENCE.

| IDENTIFY A LIMITING BELIEF | CATEGORY: ABILITY, SOCIAL INFLUENCES, SELF-WORTH | EVIDENCE/SOURCE | | |
|---|---|---|---|---|
| EXAMPLE: "MONEY IS THE ROOT OF ALL EVIL" -"IF I GET TOO RICH, PEOPLE WILL THINK I'M A JERK" | SOCIAL+ ABILITY | DONALD TRUMP (?) | | |
| ALTERNATIVE EVIDENCE AND/OR ALTERNATIVE PARADIGMS AN INTERPRETATION THAT EMPOWERS YOU! | REINFORCEMENT: WHAT ACTION, COMMUNICATION OR SYSTEM WILL YOU PUT IN PLACE TO REINFORCE YOUR NEW, EMPOWERING BELIEFS? | | BY WHEN | DONE! |
| EXAMPLE: - TRUMP PAID OFF THE MORTGAGE FOR A GOOD DEED DOER. - MONEY CAN MAKE GREAT THINGS HAPPEN. | - INVEST IN AN EXCITING, PROFIT-BOOSTING RESOURCE (BE SPECIFIC) | | MARCH 11, 20XX | MARCH YY, 20XX |

CONTACT ME IF YOU HAVE ANY QUESTIONS OR NEED GUIDANCE, PERSPECTIVE OR SUPPORT. I'M HERE FOR YOU.

| JONATHAN FLAKS | 877.700.BOLD(2653) | WWW.JFCOACH.COM |
|---|---|---|

# STEP 1: IDENTIFY THE LIMITING BELIEF

Think about some of the limiting beliefs that came to mind as you read through the previous chapter. Did you have limiting beliefs that related to worth, social influences, or ability? For the purpose of

19

learning how to use this tool, write down one of the most salient beliefs you came up with. To make the tool work best, you will want to come up with some dramatically frank, emotional language about a barrier in your belief system. For example, "Rich people stink! I can't see myself among the filthy rich." Identify one of your limiting beliefs, describe it with words that rock you to your core, and then list it in the first box. You will get more impact from this tool if you use the most powerful language possible, because it will represent deeper beliefs that impact a broader range of your choices and habits in your life. For example, I dealt with a limiting belief that told me:

*If I become successful, I might have to travel a lot, and I prefer to be home.*

A deeper and more powerful statement for me was:

*To be successful, I'll HAVE TO travel a lot, and therefore I'll be a bad, absent parent like my father was.*

In simpler terms, the limiting belief was:

**If I'm successful, I'll FAIL as a parent.**

Can you see how this belief could limit my motivation to succeed, especially since I'm such a family man?

| **Examples of limiting beliefs:** |
|---|
| "I shouldn't have to bother with sales or marketing. I'm just good at what I do, and people will find me." |
| "I'm too old to get a new job," or "I'm washed up!" |
| "I'm too young to be taken seriously," or "I'm a joke." |
| "If I fail, I'll be humiliated in front of friends and family," or "I'm ashamed of failure." |
| "It's dangerous to be famous and in the public eye," or "If I make it, I'm a target." |
| "I'm too tired – I don't have the time or energy," or "I'm a lazy good-for-nothing." |
| "Someone like me doesn't deserve success," or "I'm not worthy of success." |

> "You have to come from money to make money."
> "The love of money is the root of all evil."
> "Career success and a solid intimate relationship don't go together
>      — one HAS TO suffer."
> "Nobody will support my ideas — nobody understands."
> "Rich people are assholes ... I never want to be an asshole."

Pick one or create one that represents your deepest concern, and put it in the first box.

(By the way, I know now that my Dad wasn't all that bad, and he sure cared a lot and did his best to give us a good life. I have also managed to keep my travel schedule balanced with lots of quality time with my wife and kids, and the concern no longer holds me back.)

## STEP 2: CATEGORIZE THE LIMITING BELIEF

The purpose of this section is to reflect and get a better handle on your limiting beliefs. The process is simple. You identify which category *your* limiting belief falls under: Is it primarily a belief about your ability level (what you can do or handle), social influences (what you think is allowed or appropriate), or self-worth (your sense of what you deserve)? The greater your awareness of a limiting belief, the more *you* have *it* and the less *it* has *you*. The more you understand it, the better your ability will be to gain control over it and, eventually, let it go.

Why bother with this categorization? Well, just imagine you never knew the differences between vans, minivans, and SUVs, and then suddenly they were pointed out to you. Suddenly, you'd have a greater awareness of the functional distinctions. This kind of simple awareness could lead you to better decisions about, say, renting or buying a minivan. Greater awareness of your limiting beliefs won't completely eliminate them, but you'll be more aware of them when they show up and stop you from being your best. When you are aware that this is happening, you have more power to choose to boldly step into the growth zone and do something differently than if you were still being blindly driven by the limiting belief.

You might find a primary category that fits your belief best and a secondary category that also relates to your belief. It is fine to consider two categories – one primary and one secondary, because that also adds awareness. The process of considering categories focuses your mind on the subject and creates fresh awareness. For example, it's interesting to consider a belief like, "That's not the way it's done around here." Is that a social-driven belief? Is it a capability-driven belief along the lines of "I don't know how *I* can do that kind of thing around here," or is it a mix? Different insights will lead you to different actions. This kind of ranking of belief influences should give you richer results.

Enter your assessment in the second box of the Frame-Shifting Frame.

## STEP 3: IDENTIFY THE SOURCE AND EVIDENCE SUPPORTING YOUR OLD BELIEF

In this step, we explore the way that your belief, no matter how twisted or counterproductive it might be, has been absolutely true for you! Denial doesn't work! Instead, we acknowledge and leverage your power to create powerful beliefs, embracing the beliefs you created from true experiences and perspectives from the past, before we shift old patterns so *you* control your beliefs, instead of the reverse.

Ask yourself, what is the source of the belief? Who trained you to hold this belief, and in what situations? Was is mother, father, sister, brother, teachers, or peers? Was it in the playground, classroom, or workplace? From TV or in your home?

Next, reflect on how the belief may have been useful to you at one time. Give yourself some credit for how this belief served you well in the past. Can you see why the belief had a purpose? Identifying the source of the belief with the intention of transcending the belief as it once was once useful to you will help you relegate the belief to the past. This process helps to strip the belief of its limiting power in current and new situations.

To deepen your understanding, document what evidence or reasons you have that your belief is true. There must be plenty of evidence supporting the belief for you to believe it so firmly. Of course, sometimes we believe things without any evidence, if we want badly enough to believe them. What are your reasons for investing in this belief? The greater the insight you have into the reasons you hold your belief to be true (but not the only truth), the greater will be your ability to transcend it. If you are working with a very powerful limiting belief, it is likely that you feel that the limiting belief is truer than anything else, and therefore it is *the* truth. But that will soon change as you begin to do the rest of the frame-shifting exercise and explore other perspectives that also hold true. This is where the belief gets shifted. Write these perspectives in the third box.

## STEP 4: ASK YOURSELF WHAT *ELSE* IS TRUE?

If we yearn to explore life beyond the confines of our self-made limits, then we must ask ourselves, "What *else* is true?" Let's look at alternate evidence and then alternate paradigms.

An example that I love about how alternate evidence can create empowering beliefs is the story of the Beatles. Before the Fab Four were signed to their first contract, they were rejected by every major record company in the UK—an experience they could have viewed as pretty convincing evidence that nobody gave a damn about a bunch of hyped-up mop-tops from Liverpool. However, one important person *did* give a damn —their manager, Brian Epstein—and *his* belief in them was all the evidence they needed to keep shooting for a deal. In September of 1962, George Martin recorded the Beatles first hit, "Love Me Do" at Abbey Road Studios, and history was made.

You should always ask, "What *else* is true?" What evidence exists that indicates you *can* achieve a greater level of success than you have imagined? What other evidence can you find that *contradicts* the evidence supporting your limiting beliefs?

One of my clients is an actress in Hollywood who was afraid of big-time success because she also wanted healthy romantic and family relationships. Her limiting belief was *Hollywood actors and actresses don't have healthy relationships.* Now, there certainly are dozens of spectacular examples of publicized evidence to support that theory, including Alec Baldwin with Kim Basinger, Tom Cruise with Nicole Kidman, Charlie Sheen with Denise Richards, and Brad Pitt with Jennifer Aniston, to name a few. However, there are also examples of successful marriages in the entertainment business: Will and Jada Pinkett Smith, Tom Hanks and Rita Wilson, and the late, great Paul Newman and Joanne Woodward. So even if there are ten failed marriages for every one that works, the fact of the matter is that *some* do succeed, and *that's* the evidence my client believes in. It's not just a matter of cultivating optimism. Focusing on the successful couples will help her identify how they did it and how she can, too.

Next, let's look at alternate paradigms. What if there is not enough evidence to truly convince yourself that your limiting belief is untrue? There are still many other ways — alternate paradigms — of looking at the same situation. After all, you determine what you believe about most situations, anyway. So why not make up something that empowers you? For example, maybe having a single lifelong marriage isn't the only recipe for happiness. While it's true that many successful Hollywood stars fail at maintaining lifelong marriages, so do fifty percent of all Americans. So maybe an alternate paradigm for my Hollywood actress client would be, "Let me give my career the best shot I can, and, along the way, give my all to have the best possible marriage. I'll make it work as long as possible, but if at some point it is meant to come to an end, I'll be grateful for the good times, and move on!" People find happiness in many ways. A failed first marriage isn't ideal, but it isn't the end of the world, either. Both parties could end up very happy, and perhaps wiser, too. So, look at your challenge and find other points of view that are *also* true—*and* that empower you. Write your new perspective in the fourth box of the frame.

## STEP 5: REINFORCE THE FRAME SHIFT

It is vital to *reinforce* new beliefs so they become new habits of thought. Remember, you are building a new mental and emotional pathway and must keep reinforcing it until it replaces the old one. Decide on actions you can take to move something forward that will reinforce your new belief, and make a plan to sustain a new practice for at least 30 days. Consider who you can ask to help you reinforce the new belief and ask away. What can you structure in your *environment* as a reminder and support system for the new belief? These implementations represent the difference between just saying you're going to change and actually making lasting changes.

Write it down in box 5 AND on your calendar…

## STEP 6: SET A DATE

Next, make a time commitment as to when you will make the change and practice reinforcing the new belief. When you have transcended the old belief and have the change ingrained and integrated into your life, you're done! You'll either have completely overcome the old limitation and will find yourself naturally propelled forward, or you'll at least find yourself more aware when your limiting belief is holding you back, and with that awareness, you'll be able to make mental frame shifts and consider new perspectives on the spot. You will have already done the heavy lifting and learned the skill.

Whenever you succeed, take some time to enjoy the confidence and success that your growth has brought. Very successful, balanced people grow, then plateau for some time, and then seek to grow more. As the Dalai Lama said, "It is wise to live 100% content with who you are and where you are on your path...*and* have just enough ambition to keep things interesting." Each time you work through this process, you expand yourself beyond past limitations. I recommend you apply this process toward your goals for success, happiness, relationships, and finances. For best results, work through at least two or three limiting beliefs during your first month with this book. Start now and you'll begin to feel more successful immediately.

## SHORTCUT

Is there something that you want to achieve or a step you want to take that you have been procrastinating? Imagine that you absolutely MUST figure out a way to move forward or else ... no alternative, no backup, and no safety net!

What beliefs or circumstances do think are holding you back?

_____

_____

_____

What else is true? What perspective can you believe that would empower you?

_____

_____

_____

What resources could you leverage, and how?

_____

_____

_____

Who can help if you just ask? Who can you ask to keep you accountable?

_____

_____

_____

What will you do, by when, to get moving forward?

_____

_____

Write down the answers to all of the preceding questions. Practice this exercise for one specific situation right now.

If this shortcut works for you, make this thought process a new practice that you'll employ on a regular basis. For best results, create a journal of challenges you face. Document how you attack the issues with your powerful creativity and resourcefulness, simply using what was already within your reach *and* just out of your reach – the things you are able to grasp when you S-T-R-E-T-C-H!

---

### Challenge Homework

Identify one or two limiting beliefs or challenges and work through the frame-shifting frame one issue at a time. If you already were doing this when reading the chapter, do it again with another limiting belief. Do a few of them until you get really good at turning a draining, negative, limiting belief on its ear and replacing it with an inspiring, motivating belief that leads you to take action with ease and excitement. For extra value and some fun, share this concept with someone you trust, and guide each other through some frame-shifting conversations.

---

# Chapter 4
# The Comfort Zone and Growth Zone

*"The only way of discovering the limits of the possible is to venture a little way past them into the impossible.*
*– Arthur Clarke, science fiction writer*

Personal growth is rarely simple or easy. If it were, you probably would have done what you needed to do long ago. In addition, we have a tendency to want to stick with what's known and comfortable, perhaps without even realizing that we're avoiding the growth we crave. Meaningful growth almost always involves moving out of what is familiar and comfortable and into a zone that is just the opposite – unfamiliar and uncomfortable. It is not an easy process. If you want your life to progress differently than it has in the last few years, you will have to go beyond what is usual and cozy. You will have to approach some aspects of your life quite differently than you have before and, by definition; it is quite uncomfortable outside the "comfort zone." Sometimes it is even frightening and debilitating to consider new ways of thinking and acting, even if you are enthusiastic about the ideas.

Much has been written and discussed regarding the comfort zone. It is the collective circumstances and pursuits within which we usually feel most calm, satisfied, safe, and in control, because we are engaged in what is familiar. Most people spend most of their time in their comfort zone *because* it is predictable. Many remain there even when they feel sad, bored, depressed, and lonely, simply because they need that sense of control.

There's nothing wrong with living in the comfort zone. However, most human beings thrive on growth, and it is more invigorating, healthy, and satisfying to be growth-oriented. Growth happens when we challenge our limitations and get outside our comfort zone. Therefore, it may take extra courage to deal with the anxiety, uneasiness, and doubt that comes with change.

Everyone has heard the phrase "Step out of your comfort zone." The Comfort Zone Map (see Figure 2 below) will help you visualize the zone and manage the feelings of taking bold steps and leaps forward. If you step outside the comfort zone, you are, by definition, exploring areas of the unknown. Most everything we attempt that is unfamiliar is, at first, uncomfortable. So when you try things that are new and different, and therefore unknown, consider with some excitement that this is the growth zone.

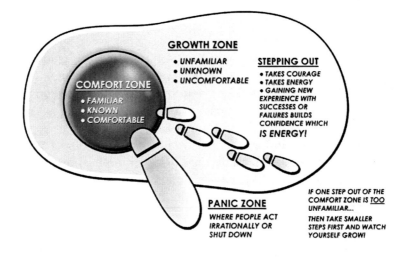

**Figure 2.** The Comfort Zone Map.

Procrastination is the most common byproduct of avoiding discomfort and being stuck in the comfort zone. People choose to procrastinate and allow themselves to be distracted —yes, that's right, it is a choice—because a task or conversation is uncomfortable, onerous, distasteful, or downright scary. Haven't you found yourself putting off things you know you should do? It's usually because you just can't bring yourself to face the challenge. Write down something here that you have been putting off because it seems to be outside your comfort zone:

_____

_____

## GIANT STEPS

It takes some courage to step out of the comfort zone, but that is where the growth happens. You will either achieve a desired result and celebrate your victory, or you'll fall short of the desired result and make a choice; either chalk it up as a failure, or learn and grow. If you choose to celebrate your effort anyway, choosing to learn and grow regardless of the outcome, you can't lose, and you always grow. The learning and experience you gain is invaluable as you take courageous actions, initiate new relationships, explore new beliefs, and engage in new experiences. As these things occur, your comfort zone grows to include your new experiences as familiar, no-longer-uncharted territory. You gain greater confidence in the new area and thereby expand the scope of what you are willing and able to face.

What happens if you push too far away from the comfort zone? If you attempt (or even contemplate) something that is too unknown or too foreign, you may find yourself in the panic zone. People who venture into the panic zone usually react in one of two ways: They shut down completely and retreat in terror to the middle of their comfort zone, or they act out feelings of frustration, confusion, despair, or shock in other irrational ways ranging from impulsiveness and stupidity to rage, hostility, or even self-sabotage.

Therefore, it is important to be aware of the terrain between your comfort zone and the panic zone, so you can recognize your own emotional signals and manage the challenges in the growth zone that keep you growing, rather than pushing TOO hard and having it back-fire.

## BABY STEPS

What happens if you do want to grow but even a single step be-yond your usual approach feels like a paralyzing visit to the panic zone? If you are overwhelmed by the thought of one whole step in the direction you want to go, consider taking a partial baby step. Ask yourself, "What is a smaller or partial action I could take to move forward and build up some courage and confidence?" If writing a proposal is scary, what if you just started with a rough outline? If the thought of calling an influential contact is too intimidating and causes you to feel nauseous or simply dismiss the idea yet again, how about looking up the telephone number and practicing the conversation in a role-play with a friend or coach?

What if you realize you need to hire someone in order to reach your goals, but you have never yet been comfortable hiring or manag-ing a person in such a position? Try breaking down the hiring process into steps:

- Create a list of criteria for the ideal person.
- Turn that list into a long Help Wanted ad.
- Email that list to people you know and trust and request suggestions for candidates, as well as advice on how to find (and manage) the right person.

Each of these three steps can move you in the right direction, and none of them would take very much time. A lot of baby steps taken in succession can yield a large leap of forward progress. Every step, no matter how small, helps your inner circle/comfort zone grow and pushes the panic zone farther out too, creating a wider margin for fur-ther growth.

Here's another example in action. When a good friend of mine, let's call him Rick, started his law career working as a legislative aide, he was terrified of public speaking. (According to one study, most people are more afraid of public speaking than of death. Noting this fact, comedian Jerry Seinfeld once quipped that most people would rather be in the coffin than delivering the eulogy!) Rick decided that he wanted to overcome his fear and believed he could. So he began taking some baby steps toward getting more comfortable with public speaking.

First, he practiced by making presentations in front of small groups. The very first baby step was at an informal gathering of a few interested voters in the home of a supporter. He was terrified, as always, but allowed himself to consider what it would feel like to get through it. He did make a presentation and reported that the response was positive and encouraging. Then, he stepped up to mixed groups of ten or twelve people who shared the interests of his legislator. Relatively quickly, he was able to get more and more comfortable making presentations to larger and larger groups. Over the course of a year, he became so comfortable he was able to *lead* discussions in front of legislative committees, including gatherings of the press and general public of over 200 people. Ultimately, speaking in public became something that he looks forward to with eagerness - today it is one of his strong suits.

All of the work in this book requires some new thinking and actions. The implementation of new choices may be unfamiliar at first and therefore somewhat uncomfortable. Scary. Dizzying. Exciting. Overwhelming. If you are prepared to experience these emotions over time, it will become easier to expand your comfort zone and grow, thereby developing new abilities and embrace new possibilities. You'll also enjoy – on purpose – the full range of emotions that human beings have been blessed with!

## JUMPING IN

Here is another concept that will help you get comfortable with stepping outside the comfort zone. I call it the "one-minute-and-forty-five-second-principle." The best way to understand it is via a metaphor.

Think about the awful feeling you get when you jump into a coldwater lake. I happen to be a passionate swimmer, scuba diver, and sailor—an all-around waterfront guy. But when it comes to that first immersion into any cold water, I simply turn chicken. I hate the bone-chilling surge on my body when the water is anything less than 77 degrees. I dip my toe, wrap my arms around myself, and shiver. If I didn't love the water so much, I'd *never* jump in. But I always remember the "1:45 Principle." I muster up some energy and courage and jump right in. I feel absolutely awful for the first minute and forty-five seconds; I hoot and holler in agony. But then, after I move around for a bit, kicking my legs and thrashing my arms, I feel invigorated, energized, and ready to swim around comfortably with freedom and joy.

The same can be said for new experiences that are uncomfortable at first. At first you hoot and holler, but if you keep moving (growing, adapting), you'll get acclimated quickly.

Another example comes from a woman named Cassie, who loved to sing and play her guitar but avoided the spotlight in every way. She rarely even played for her own family, and she became a quivering mass of jelly at merely the thought of playing in public. For thirty-five years, she sang and played a large repertoire of songs alone in her bedroom with the door closed. Then, one night she met a woman in a restaurant, a working musician, who prodded her into coming to an informal jam session at a local café. She convinced Cassie, after much resistance, to play a couple of songs for a small group of amateur musicians who were there to jam. She agreed, reluctantly, and it took all the courage she could find to get on stage. But she played and sang well and got good feedback. She was encouraged to come back for the next jam. She did. She played again and got good feedback again. She continued going to the jams, started singing with more confidence, and, as a result, started sounding even better. And the feedback got even better. After a few months, she was willing to perform for the relatively few patrons who came to that restaurant on weeknights. But she always sat in a chair and was largely hidden behind her music stand as she performed. One Saturday night, she agreed (against her better judgment) to fill in for the paid entertainer who had to cancel at the last minute, and she played for a full house. Eventually, she learned to play standing up and memorized her repertoire so she could dispense with the music stand.

Six months after this all started, she was invited to join a new rock band. A year after that, the band has really taken off, and now she sings regularly at the top of her lungs in front of crowds of people for hours at a time. She still sings at the café twice a month, as well as at other venues. She now can't imagine going more than two weeks without standing in front of a microphone looking out at people watching her sing. Two years ago, she would have said, "Never in a million years would it be possible for me to do any of these things." What a journey? She did it through a series of baby steps that just kept growing larger and larger all the time.

Courage *takes* energy, but action and learning with the right attitude turns *every* experience, including setbacks, into confidence, and confidence *is* energy. So, keep feeding your system with courage and action and take every challenge you can with a passion for learning opportunities. You will develop new levels of confidence that will last you a lifetime.

Now that you have taken on your limiting beliefs and minimized their repressive effects and also learned to stretch yourself out of your comfort zone, it is time to start thinking BIG. The next step is to come up with your vision for what you want your life to be like. Remember, you have one life to live. Make it be all that it can be.

---

### Challenge Homework

1. Write a paragraph about something that was very scary and uncomfortable at first but became easier after you gave it a few tries. Write about it with reference to all five senses, if at all possible. What did you see at first? What did it feel like at first, and how did the feeling change? How did you come to see things differently?
2. Draw a picture of your own comfort zone map and place some words that represent steps you might take to have your income double with half the trouble. What are the giant steps that excite you most? What are the baby steps that will move you forward in a direction that you otherwise found too uncomfortable?

---

# Chapter 5

# Creating Your Vision

*Vision without action is a daydream. Action without vision is a nightmare.*

*—Japanese proverb*

If you have been taking in some of the ideas outlined in the preceding chapters, you may already be moving forward with a different attitude and momentum. It may be subtle, but you already are beginning to see new opportunities, finding hidden creative abilities and energy, or gaining confidence and motivation to move in a very successful direction. Can you see and feel it working already? To reinforce that feeling and build on it, write a few lines about what you've been experiencing here.

_____

_____

_____

_____

_____

_____

Consider emailing your new views to a few friends to reinforce what you've been learning—people who will be happy for you and perhaps be inspired to follow your example.

The purpose of this chapter is to help you clarify a meaningful purpose from your heart's desire that will inspire you to create a plan for a great life. I recommend that you engage in every section of this chapter to create a memorable experience and the most efficient map for your unique goals.

Now that you have directed the foundation of your belief system to make your income double with half the trouble and you've buckled your emotional seat belt, let's talk about a crystal clear goal that you can believe in so you know precisely what target you are shooting for.

So far, the only goal we've addressed is the one described by the title of this book—having your income double with half the trouble in one year. However, at this stage, it is mainly a concept and doesn't engage any of your senses. "Half the trouble" still focuses on the trouble, which may be all you currently see and feel. Income double may just be a number in your mind, not a vision of your new reality.

A powerful vision and a clear description of specific goals engage all the senses. If you can imagine what you would see, hear, smell, taste, and feel in your life when your income doubles with half the trouble, you are more likely to move toward that outcome. Let's test that theory. Imagine you have an additional $80,000 in the bank. Just imagine you see that number on the ATM screen. Got it? Good.

Now, imagine that you use that money to pay some bills, buy some things you've always wanted, plan a trip, and have some fun. Imagine with all your senses. What do you see, smell, taste, hear, and feel?

For example, imagine this morning that you purchased a fantastic new car in your favorite color, and you step into that new car smell, taking a sip of extra-fine-roast coffee before putting your high-tech thermos into the new cup holder. As you turn the ignition and hear the purr of the engine over the sound system playing your favorite music, you feel that thrill of success. Doesn't it engage you more than just imagining the number on the ATM screen? Isn't it more emotional? If you would do something different with an extra $80,000, imagine your choices with all five senses.

In this chapter you will develop your vision statement and a set of goals. Vision statements have become ubiquitous since Peter Drucker and others popularized them in the 1980s as a way for companies to articulate their highest purpose. About 85 percent of large companies worldwide have them. They provide a common goal to inspire and galvanize an otherwise diverse array of employees, particularly for global companies.

A personal vision statement can provide you with something concrete to believe in and get inspired by, based on your true heart's desire. What could be more inspiring than having clear goals for an ideal life and your own sense of purpose behind those goals? Your vision is within you and can be brought out through your imagination. With a visualization of your ideal life, you can distill that vision down to a few key themes and goals. Playing for what you really want your life to be about provides a sense of passion and purpose, which has proven to be a key ingredient for meaningful happiness.

Ideally you will set a big goal and go for it. If it is a big stretch for you, that is good, because it will push you to expand your creativity and resourcefulness and therefore uncover solutions and relationships that you may not otherwise discover. Life is tough no matter what, so you might as well put your energy toward the biggest dream possible, with clear goals to shoot for along the way.

## VISUALIZING YOUR IDEAL FUTURE

This exercise is from the workshop I developed called "Who Are You, Inc. — Bringing Out Your Best in Business," during which I guide people to write down a version of an ideal future. The program is also available as a "seminar on CD" through my website, www.jfvisionquest.com. For best results, set yourself up for at least two sessions of self-guided coaching, one or two hours each session. Make sure you are in a comfortable environment with no distractions. Follow the instructions carefully over the course of two sessions.

### Step 1: Get Your Heart Pumping

Put on some upbeat music and get your heart rate up. Dance, jump up and down, run in place, and do jumping-jacks or whatever aerobic action you choose to get your heart pumping. This clears your head and body so you can focus on your heart's desire.

39

Get your heart rate up for at least the first five minutes of your self-guided program.

## Step 2: Center Yourself

Next, put yourself in a very relaxed, comfortable, happy state of mind and body. Sit down in a comfortable chair or on the floor or wherever you want to be. Start by taking a deep, cleansing breath—in through your nose and out through your mouth—as deep as possible. Do two or three more cleansing breaths like that—as deep as possible, in through your nose and out through your mouth.

Then, allow yourself to breathe as deeply as is **comfortable** - find your own rhythm and your own pace. Put all of your attention on your breathing and the feeling of the air moving in and out of your lungs.

Allow yourself to see and feel each inhale as an input of nourishment and positive, confident energy to every cell in your body. As you exhale, let go and release, allowing your shoulders, muscles, and fingers to let go of stress and tension. Continue breathing this way for the duration of the exercise.

Notice what you see: any changing sights, light and color, depth and distance, and watch the images. If you close your eyes, notice the visualizations of your thoughts as they come, and then let each one them drift off as another one comes in.

Listen to the sounds you hear. Notice the sounds and listen for their sources. Enjoy the silence in the background.

Now, allow your mind to take a tour of your sense of touch. Feel the clothing on your body and the sensations on your skin. Allow your mind to become aware of any sensations in your body. There might be things you like, and there might be things you don't, but enjoy the feeling of just being aware of your feelings right now. Notice yourself noticing all of this, like you are observing yourself in this state, and appreciate how present and peaceful you feel right now.

Now, let's go to another level. I call this the "mini vacation." Remain present to your five senses, and imagine yourself soaring off to a distant horizon. You are on your way to an ideal vacation spot—someplace you've been to or have dreamed of going to –real or imaginary. Allow yourself to float there and land in the most comfortable, delightful, enjoyable place you can possibly imagine. Just enjoy what you see, hear, feel, and smell.

Turn your head and look to the left. Look at what you see and observe it in greater detail. Then slowly scan to the right and take it all in.

Notice what you feel on your face and how it feels to have that feeling on your face. Feel and smell the air and sense what you're sensing. Take it all in and enjoy it.

Listen to the sounds of this place. To make it all that more real, allow yourself to hear the sounds that might occur. Notice how your body feels. Enjoy how great it feels to be here, where you are, right now.

Is anyone else here with you? Is there a drink or anything to eat being served? Allow yourself to explore that, smell it, taste it, touch it. And smile. It feels so good to be here.

It has been proven that the mind and body cannot distinguish between real and imagined sensory experiences. Take as long as you like to enjoy the experience of being on your imaginary vacation. When you are ready, we will save this image. Imagine you can capture the experience in a little, clear glass ball you can hold between your thumb and forefinger. See yourself in that scene. Imprint this image into this little clear ball, and put it in your pocket for a moment. Now, pull it out again and jump into the experience, allowing yourself to imagine with all 5 senses that you are really there again.

So any time you're in the mood for a vacation—whether it's just to get away from stress or to center yourself and recharge your batteries for the rest of the day—I invite you to take out the imaginary glass ball and go on a mini vacation.

## Step 3: Log Into Your Heart's Desire

This next exercise is called "Your Heart's Desire," and it is designed to put you in tune with your preferences and get you warmed up to rediscover your passion. Write whatever comes to mind in response to each question.

What are your favorite foods? Think of your favorite appetizer, entrée, dessert.

_____

_____

What is your favorite movie of all time? If that's too big of a question, what is your favorite movie of recent times?

_____

Who are some of your favorite musical artists?

_____

_____

What are some of your favorite songs?

_____

_____

_____

What books have you read recently that you really loved?

_____

_____

_____

What would you do if you had plenty of extra spare time?

_____

If you could travel anywhere, where would you most like to go?

You have listed things you love—your own unique choices from your heart's desire. The point of this exercise is to make sure you are in touch with your own heart's desires and thereby help you better envision the ideal future you can strive toward.

## Step 4: Tell The Genie What You Want.

I call the next exercise "Your Genie in the Lamp." This is a process for gathering insight into who you are and what you love, what makes you tick, indeed, what makes you rock! It will be useful information for distilling your passion—your purpose—and for finding clues that may become part of your plan later.

You will be responding to a series of thought-provoking questions. Just write and keep writing whatever comes to mind. If you get stuck, look at the next question or look away and close your eyes and allow the next thought to occur, and then you'll have something to begin writing again. The more possibilities you can get on paper, the better.

You'll need plenty of room to write, so don't be restricted to the spaces I've provided in this book. For this exercise, please get some paper of your own or work on this at your computer.

Ready?

Go!

Imagine you've got a lamp like Aladdin's lamp, but the genie says, "You've got unlimited wishes, and your whole life can be a dream come true. All you have to do is ask. All you have to do is know what to ask for."

Where would you go first? It might be back to that ideal vacation we created a few moments ago. Describe it in detail.

_____

_____

_____

_____

_____

Write a little about why you'd like to go there.

_____

_____

_____

_____

_____

Now think about where you would live if you could live anywhere in the world. Describe it in detail. What would be in your environment? What would your home be like?

_____

_____

_____

_____

_____

What is it about this home that makes it home for you? How would it make you feel? Describe as much as you can about where you'd live and anything about why you'd live there.

_____

_____

_____

_____

_____

You've got unlimited freedom. What do you do with your time? What would a typical free day be like?

_____

_____

_____

_____

_____

How and when would you start your morning?

_____

_____

_____

_____

_____

What might your afternoon and midday look like?

_____

_____

_____

_____

_____

How would you transition to your evening?

_____

_____

_____

_____

_____

What would your night-time and bed time be like?

_____

_____

_____

_____

_____

In your ideal life, you get to pursue your dream career. What would you do to earn money doing things that make you happy?

_____

_____

_____

_____

_____

What makes this fun?

_____

_____

_____

_____

_____

What makes it meaningful?

_____

_____

_____

_____

_____

How does it support what you really want to contribute to the world?

_____

_____

_____

_____

_____

If you are working as part of a team, what sort of team is it? What are the people like? Look at the team you work with. What do you admire most about them as individuals?

_____

_____

_____

_____

_____

What are some of the qualities of the individuals on the team that you like?

_____

_____

_____

_____

_____

What about the team experience turns you on?

_____

_____

_____

_____

_____

What is your place in the team?

_____

_____

_____

_____

_____

How would you like to be appreciated for your contribution on the team?

_____

_____

_____

_____

_____

In an ideal week, what would you do, and on which days?

_____

_____

_____

_____

_____

How would your new, ideal life be distinctly different from your old life? What from your old life would be missing in this new life? What would you no longer have to put up with?

_____

_____

_____

_____

_____

What are the personal relationships like in your life? What kind of intimate, romantic relationship would you be in?

_____

_____

_____

_____

_____

What about your friendships and your family relationships?

_____

_____

_____

_____

_____

What is it about them that you'd admire and appreciate the most?

_____

_____

_____

_____

_____

What is it that you think they would appreciate most about you?

_____

_____

_____

_____

_____

What would you want them to appreciate most about you?

_____

_____

_____

_____

_____

With all of this freedom, what do you stand for? What do you want to be remembered for?

_____

_____

_____

_____

_____

What are some of the qualities or values that you want your life to be about? What are the values you express in this life?

_____

_____

_____

_____

_____

And if all these things were present, what else would be possible?

_____

_____

_____

_____

_____

At this point, take some time to continue writing, filling in some of the holes, expanding on some of the experiences you could see, taking this wherever you'd like it to go. If you'd like, put on some music and continue writing for an even longer time. Then, when you come back, we'll make sense of it all.

## Step 5: Distill Your Personal Vision Statement

Next, look for five things in what you wrote to sort out the clues that are most useful. For this part of the exercise, you will need a blue pen, a red pen, a yellow highlighter, and a black pencil. For best results, read each of the five sets of instructions below one at a time, and review all of your notes for each set of instructions.

1.  The first thing to do is to look for those things in your dream life that you already have in your real life, and to look at them with **gratitude**. What do you have in the description of your dream life that you already have in your real life? Take a look at your notes and draw a **blue box** around the words that describe those things. Those are the blue pearls you want to allow yourself to be grateful for every day.
2.  The second category of things to look for are those projects with **momentum**. What are the goals that you would love to accomplish in your dream life that you are already pursuing and already have some momentum toward fulfilling? Take your **red pen and circle** those, because

53

there is some urgency there. You are already in motion and may want to make your very next moves in those directions. For example, you may already be in the process of starting a business, and your dream might be to have that business be at a certain level. Your notes might contain some clues on what aspects of your business you want to focus on right away.

3. The third category is what I call **misguided notions.** Look at your goals, and think about them carefully. Are some of them there so that you can prove something, fix something, or compensate for some perceived inadequacy or deficiency? Be honest with yourself, and identify those projects that you might be driven toward but that really aren't inspiring to you. Take a **pencil and draw a line through them**. It may not be easy, but those are the ones where you want to learn to say "no."

    For example, one person I coached originally had a drive to become a serial entrepreneur. He started to spread himself too thin by pursuing all kinds of ideas. This desire did not really grow out of his own passion, but instead grew out of an ambition that he thought he needed to impress his father. He had always been pushed to do everything possible to succeed. This misunderstood philosophy was a huge source of stress and anxiety, not a source of joy, even though he was very creative. After gaining some perspective, he realized that he was happiest doing everything he could to succeed within his core niche of chiropractic care. Once he focused on this vision, he pursued it with great passion and was much more happy and successful.

4. The fourth area to explore is the realm of **possibilities**. What goals and desires do you see as possibilities worth pursuing that you may or may not have considered possible before now? Look in your notes at some dreams that might hint at big challenges along the way. Perhaps now you are more ready to choose one or two that would be fulfilling, that you could go for, that you may not have pursued in the past. **Highlight them in bright yellow** and make sure those get into your long-term planning. Be

aware that you are going to need loads of creativity and patience. Whenever you have a big goal in the game— seemingly impossible possibilities—the game becomes very challenging but much more exciting. You are more likely to experience miracles in those pursuits.

5. Finally, the fifth—and I think most valuable—set of clues are called **values.** These are your highest aspirations, words that inspire you, your purest motives, and your higher self. Some examples of that might be freedom, connectedness, contribution, and vitality. A few of mine are peace, love, adventure and fun. **Circle these words with any color you like AND highlight them in bright yellow everywhere they occur.** These words are the foundation for a future you purposefully design. These are the words that may constitute your vision.

Spend some time sorting out these clues. Have fun with your highlighter and your different colored pens, and then we'll move forward.

## "Distill Your Vision"

| Gratitude | Things already in your life | Draw a **blue** box around them |
|---|---|---|
| **Momentum** | Goals you're already working toward and may be close to achieving | Draw a **red** circle around them |
| **Misguided Notions** | What you *thought* your life should have | Strike with **pencil** |
| **Possibilities** | Dreams worth pursuing | Highlight in **yellow** |
| **Values** | The underlying purpose behind your dreams | Highlight in **yellow AND circle any color** |

## Vision Statement

Now we can begin to look at how to apply your values to your vision:

- Are you willing to allow yourself to let your passions guide your life?
- If you are, might you also be willing to have your whole life – your business and personal life – aligned toward sharing these qualities and values with the world?

If so, then your passion is indeed your purpose. Great! Now you can use any of the words that represent your values to inspire you in any or all of your communication. The more you use, identify with, share, and center yourself on your own conception of your purpose, the more you'll be living with the energy that we know as passion. This can be very inspiring, energizing, and attractive to other people, all things that lead to greater and easier success.

One of the ways businesses harness the power of these words is by creating a centralized vision statement—a statement that crystallizes the essence of their values and goals for the future. What does having a strong vision statement do? For me and for many of my clients, it helps direct action and attracts the highest forms of reward.

The following is my vision statement:

*People love what they do and do what they love, living life as an extraordinary adventure in deeply fulfilling relationships. Life is serious business – have fun with it.*

My strongest values of love, adventure, peace, fulfillment, relationships, and fun are all there. I started with identifying those values and then threaded them together to form a declaration. You may also notice that it's not just about me, but I'm included in the values I wish for all people. Your vision statement should be a combination of the expression of your values and what you'll *do* in terms of the dream goal you will pursue and how you'll be an inspiration for others – that way your vision will attract people who share your vision and may want to support your goals. Your vision statement can include a dream that's impossible in your lifetime but worth striving for nonetheless.

Now, take a crack at stringing together the words you have that are a powerful expression of your values. Don't try to get this perfect right away. Start with a rough draft. For best results, put on your favorite music while you write. Then edit it to create a coherent, well-worded vision statement that sums up how you want to live your life. This is an important step and, I confess, very hard to do alone. Most people struggle over getting the right words in the right order, rewriting it more than a few times and risk dropping it before it has a chance to be meaningful and useful. This is one of those times when it is worthwhile to spend an hour with a coach to talk it through, get it out in the open, get objective, unbiased but inspiring feedback and leverage some linguistic expertise. If you need any support on this step, feel free to contact me by phone or e-mail to arrange a coaching session with me or one of my vision statement experts on my team.

Once you have it down just right, put it to use. Don't hide it or forget about it. Stick it on the wall or print it on the back of your business cards. Put it on your email signature. See what happens in your life when you tell people what you stand for.

In the next chapter, we'll begin the planning process for achieving your ideal life. Planning involves setting big goals and specifying the milestones along the way. When you know what you want to accomplish, what actions you're going to take, and what results you're looking to achieve over time, you'll be better able to track your progress and enjoy your victories.

Think bigger and you'll grow faster.

---

### Challenge Homework

Distill your passion and purpose to a vision statement and commit to living every day with those values.

---

# Part II:
## Delete

One of the simplest ways to have your income double with half the trouble is to start by cutting out the trouble. It makes sense: how can you maximize your capacity for attracting income when you have obstacles in your way? Certainly, there are some challenges that you have no control over. Have you ever heard of the old "serenity" prayer? The basic version goes like this:

"God, grant me

the serenity to accept the things I cannot change,
the courage to change the things I can,
and the wisdom to know the difference."

I've created an alternative version:

*"Infinite power (whatever you believe in,) please* grant me:
the serenity to accept *and embrace* the things I cannot change;
the courage, *creativity, and resourcefulness* to change the things I can,
and the wisdom to know the difference."

Now that we believe in and are working toward having your income double, we need to create a framework and clear the way for it to actually happen. Part II gives you the tools for getting rid of obstacles that you may not even realize are interfering with your income, success, and happiness.

In Part I, you explored how and why your beliefs are structured the way they are, and how you can change them to better yourself and achieve your goals. Now you need to focus on your environment—specifically, on how to take action (including communication) to make the changes you want and need to make.

The components of your environment include:

- *tools and technology you have access to*
- *the décor of your work and living space*
- *resources and relationships around you*
- *the systems and methods you use to get things done*

These collective aspects of your environment could be represented simply by boxes in the following graphic:

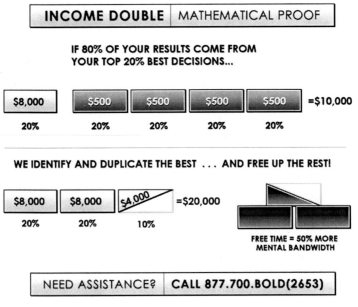

**INCOME DOUBLE** | MATHEMATICAL PROOF

**IF 80% OF YOUR RESULTS COME FROM
YOUR TOP 20% BEST DECISIONS...**

| $8,000 | $500 | $500 | $500 | $500 | =$10,000 |
| 20% | 20% | 20% | 20% | 20% | |

**WE IDENTIFY AND DUPLICATE THE BEST . . . AND FREE UP THE REST!**

| $8,000 | $8,000 | $4,000 | =$20,000 |
| 20% | 20% | 10% | |

**FREE TIME = 50% MORE
MENTAL BANDWIDTH**

NEED ASSISTANCE? | **CALL 877.700.BOLD(2653)**

Voila! If your goal is to have your income double with half the trouble, you eliminate the most wasteful blocks and focus on the most fruitful areas of your environment that are worth leveraging. Each of the grey boxes represents some aspect of your world that is not optimal. One of those boxes could, for example, represent the 20% of your environment that is responsible for 80% of your headaches! The other three boxes represent below average resources that you have put up with, mediocrity that you have accepted, and even some choices that are good, but not great.

Should you give it all up at once in order to make room for excellence? That may be too extreme an approach, but some people have the luxury of a fast track purge. Most people who are successful with this exercise, however, will integrate a process of replacing things over time. You may be better off moving step by step toward an extraordinary life and lifestyle in a way that doesn't jeopardize your basic survival needs or the integrity you manage by honoring existing commitments.

Your environment is currently organized to yield the life you have now. The task at hand is to create an environment organized to produce your future. If you change your current environment, you change your future.

Start today! Rid yourself of anything that drains your energy. Chapter 6 will kick-start the process by helping you eliminate some energy-draining distractions from your environment, such as clutter and nagging chores.

Chapter 7 will help you focus by reducing over-involvement and over-commitment.

Rise above the below-average relationships that don't further your goals. Be done with mediocrity—for good! Chapter 8 helps you set boundaries with people who drain your energy or mistreat you.

And Chapter 9 gets you to raise your standards, so you say, "No, thank you" to merely *good* involvements and instead engage in *great* investments.

As you engage in these chapters, take on the challenge homework suggestions with great gusto and commitment and you will soon cut your trouble in half (or better).

Have fun with this energizing process!

# Chapter 6
# Clearing Away the Clutter

*"You are a product of your environment. So choose the environment that will best develop you toward your objective. Analyze your life in terms of its environment. Are the things around you helping you toward success - or are they holding you back?"*
*- W. Clement Stone*

You may not be fully aware of it, but you are tolerating more unnecessary drains in your daily life than you should. There are lots of little things around you that make you go, "Uggggh." Each one by itself might not be a big deal, but put enough of them together in a day and you're likely to become aggravated, frustrated, annoyed, drained, and certainly not your best self. Most of us ignore the little dysfunctions in our environment; a loose doorknob or squeaky door, windshield wipers that need replacing, disorganized papers, a messy closet, and other annoying situations. The fact is, you've created or allowed many of these energy drains to exist in your life, and they interfere with your success and fulfillment.

You know you can do something about these drains, but if you're like most people, you procrastinate or just let them slide. And procrastinating just makes the problems worse. If you don't act, many energy drains pile up until you feel overwhelmed.

Now is the time, as part of this program, for you to eliminate your energy drains and de-clutter, one thing at a time, step-by-step, in order to recapture your full energy, to become more effective and focused, and to start attracting more of what you desire. Like any exercise, it may take some time from your life, but it will allow you to have more life in your time.

Using the chart below, make a list of the energy drains in your environment. * Examples might be a tree limb that needs to be cut down, an unfinished bathroom in your house that requires you to find a new contractor, or personal finance files that are disorganized and cause you distress whenever you need to find an important document.

Next, decide what you need to do to make this trouble go away. If you have a wall that has gotten old and a bit dirty, will you paint it, clean it, or hang a picture over the most visible stain? Do you need to assign some time to reorganizing your files or your desk?

OR

Now that you have experience with "frame-shifting," decide a new way of looking at something that was once "trouble," but is not a problem if you think about it differently. For example, you might notice that your client's parking lot is always full, and you have to park pretty far to get to the entrance. You can't change that, but you can embrace the fact that there are always a lot of customers at your client's site, which is good for their business and, therefore, good for you. You can also decide to enjoy the extra exercise you get every time you have to walk to and from your car.

For each item that you determine must be changed, create a specific, measurable solution to be implemented over a period of time. Don't try to do everything at once. Decide on a date by which you will have resolved each issue, either by taking action to make a change, or to reframe how you interpret the situation, and enter that date into the third column of the chart.

---

**Energy Drain Chart**

◇ Top 10 Energy Drains ◇ Change or Embrace It? ◇ By When? ◇

1._____
2._____
3._____
4._____
5._____
6._____
7._____
8._____
9._____
10._____

---

*This material is inspired and influenced by concepts created by Thomas Leonard as presented in training programs at Coach University, as well as in his book "The Portable Coach."

You can tackle these energy drains, item by item, one or a few at a time. You may begin to experience benefits from this process as soon as you start planning your action. When you decide to eliminate an energy drain and have a plan to do so, you immediately begin to *feel* as though the problem is solved simply because you are taking charge of your life, and that is empowering!

One client of mine who engaged in this simple exercise decided he needed to tackle his messy work space at his office. His desk was a disaster by most people's standards. He knew that HE could find what he needed most of the time without an unreasonable amount of hunting, but when we discussed the list of energy drains, he confessed that he was aggravated by how his desk looked. So after a coaching session, he spent a half day cleaning up, putting things away, and making files, and thus created a whole new work environment. He later reported that he received a promotion and a healthy raise even though he had been told that the other person in the running was more likely to get the promotion. He told me, "I'm quite sure my boss noticed the reorganizing of my desk space and my newly recharged energy."

The way to fill up your list of energy drains is to take a walking tour / mental tour of your environment. Start with your desk, your files, your closets, and your car. In your personal life, scan your bedroom, your bathroom, kitchen, foyer, living room, dining room, garage, etc. The more you identify and handle, the more freedom and energy you will recapture!

Consider your closet, for example. Get rid of stuff that you haven't worn in a year and that you know you will probably never wear. Eliminate 30% to 50% of the space-wasters in your closet, and enjoy the ease with which you can find the good stuff now that it isn't all crammed in there. Then you'll get the idea. I got rid of five bags of clothing once and found some terrific, virtually brand new shirts in the depths of my closet!

Set a deadline of one month (or whatever seems reasonable) to take care of all of these "material" energy drains in your environment. Tackle the items one at a time. Every day from now until that deadline, get up in the morning, look at your list, and make progress on one or more of your energy drains. Then, cross each one off the list after you've succeeded in conquering it. (This is an important step because it is so satisfying.) Reward yourself when you have managed to cross a pre-set number of energy drains off your list!

---

**Challenge Homework**

Create a specific list of energy drains that are within your control and the means by which you will eliminate them. Then handle at least three of them for starters. It's easy if you break things down into manageable steps! Set a goal to tackle a specific number of energy drains within thirty days and see what happens. Follow through with reasonable goals and timelines so you cut at least half of your troubles from your life.

---

# Chapter 7

# Reducing Over-Involvement

*"Until you value yourself, you won't value your time. Until you value your time, you will not do anything with it."*
*– M. Scott Peck, psychiatrist and writer*

You know your type. If the title of this chapter calls to you, you are probably super involved and often overwhelmed. (If you're not, you could skim this chapter and move on to the next.)

The good news is you are most likely well-intentioned, caring, and ambitious, and you want to make the world a better place. Your heart is in the right place. The bad news is you have too much on your plate, and you're spreading yourself too thin. You push yourself to meetings or force yourself to deal with tasks or people that may not excite you or be valuable anymore. You are not as effective as you hope to be, yet you don't pull out and move on.

Maybe you don't want to hurt anyone's feelings. Perhaps the word "no" is not in your everyday vocabulary. Maybe you don't believe anyone can do what you do, and you secretly fear the big project will crumble without you. Or maybe you don't have faith that fewer involvements can be equally fulfilling. You want to "do good," but by trying to do too much, you never end up feeling like it's good enough!

You're not alone. Millions of entrepreneurs and professionals incessantly over-commit. However, overextension leads to stress and limits your ability to apply your energy to its fullest potential.

While many people suffer from this circumstance, very few people do anything about it. They get stuck and stay there. Not you – not anymore - you're committed to having a great life, not just a busy one.

Now is the time to take inventory of your involvements and make proactive choices about your life and time management. The Involvements Inventory tool enables you to systematically analyze your activities so you can make better decisions about how to spend your time.

Make a list of your commitments and enter them into the chart on page 72 I'm talking about all the things you make time for. This could include making time with clients, marketing projects, reading e-mails, and surfing the internet. This could also include activities you volunteer for, such as PTA, community work, running the book club, etc.

When you have a thorough list, go over the list and rate the value these activities hold for you in each of several different categories, using a scale from -10 to 10, with 10 being most positive, 0 being neutral, and -10 being most negative. The categories you need to consider are as follows:

- **Time Expended:** Rate the amount of time you spend on the activity, relative to the other activities, as a negative number. The more time you spend, the closer the number should be to -10. If you have any involvements that are exquisitely streamlined or perfectly efficient, they should score closest to 10.

- **Financial Cost/Gain:** Rate the net cost or gain of the activity as either the negative or positive number accordingly. For instance, perhaps you spend money on gas and tolls to get to this activity. Consider what it costs you to take time away from your business to engage in this activity. If the cost is insignificant (a few dollars now and again), rate it something like a -1. If the cost is more substantial—for instance, maybe you have to spend $1000 every few months on tickets for the fundraisers for causes you are involved in—rate it more like a -8. If the activity clearly leads to financial gain and puts money in your account, the score should be a positive number. The greater the income, the higher the score!

- **Difficulty - Energy Drained vs. Energy Gained:** Rate the amount of effort, struggle, and trouble you feel each commitment takes from you. If it is draining, enter a negative number. If it is not draining, enter 0. If it energizes you and plays on your best skills and talents, give it a positive number.

- **Emotional Drain or Gain:** Rate how emotionally satisfying or unsatisfying you feel the activity is for you, with either a positive or a negative number. Some activities, such as those you engage in to support clubs or sports that your children are involved in, might have very high emotional value, even if you get anxious before or during the big games!

- **Relevant Learning or Experience:** Rate how the activity adds to your skill set and/or might support your goals and vision. For instance, chairing a committee for a community group might be providing you with valuable leadership experience and contacts that you can leverage in your business career. The rating should be 0 or a positive number.

- **Other:** You can put any subject that is important to you as a column heading. For example, some activities might help you increase your visibility and influence in your community, while others might be centered around building up assets or other forms of benefits for you in the future. A school related involvement, for example, might have value in giving you the chance to get to know other parents and teachers and have some influence over your child's educational experience. You choose and create the categories that matter most to YOU.

By Listing And Scoring Your Involvements, You Can Gain More Perspective And Objectivity About How You Spend Your Time And Energy. Then You Can Make Decisions About How To Reduce Over-Involvement And Cut Back Or Eliminate Some Of The Lower-Scoring Activities And Give Yourself More Time To Focus On The Ones That Make The Greatest Positive Impact.

## Involvements Inventory

| Involvement Name | Time Ex- pended | $$ Cost or Gain | Difficulty: Energy Drained or Gained | Emotional Drain or Gain | Relevant Learning or Experience | Other (e.g., influence, connections, assets) | TOTAL |
|---|---|---|---|---|---|---|---|
|  |  |  |  |  |  |  |  |
|  |  |  |  |  |  |  |  |
|  |  |  |  |  |  |  |  |
|  |  |  |  |  |  |  |  |
|  |  |  |  |  |  |  |  |

Figure 3 – Involvement Inventory Template

Here's a sample Involvements Inventory for a person named Nancy:

| Involvement Name | Time Ex- pended | $$ Cost or Gain | Difficulty: Energy Drained or Gained | Emotional Drain or Gain | Relevant Learning or Experience | Other (e.g., influence, connections, assets) | TOTAL |
|---|---|---|---|---|---|---|---|
| BRN Network | -7 | 1 | -6 | 8 | 7 | 6 | 5 |
| PTA committee | -4 | 0 | -1 | 9 | 8 | 8 | 20 |
| Training Dave | -8 | -2 | 2 | 7 | 9 | 9 | 17 |
| French Lessons | -4 | -1 | -7 | -5 | 4 | 2 | -11 |
| Coordinating the Car pool | -6 | 0 | -8 | -4 | 0 | 3 | -15 |

Figure 4 – Involvement Inventory Example

Of these involvements, Nancy clearly benefits from her PTA committee for its emotional value, relative learning, and clout in the school. And she certainly benefits from training her new associate, Dave. She also sees a small net gain from being in the BRN Network, despite the drain, time expended, and cost.

If she wanted to cut her involvements in half by eliminating or reducing involvements, she could:

a) Reduce the time spent with the BRN Network or find a networking group that yields better results.
b) Delegate the carpool coordination to someone else (it's someone else's turn by now!).
c) Eliminate the French lessons she thought she "should" take to impress a particular Canadian client and trust that speaking English in that relationship is acceptable. Or she could revise her approach and simply listen to an audio program (tapes, CDs or mp3s) in the car from time to time and little by little add relevant words to her vocabulary.

Get the idea?

Now you try it. Consider listing several distinct business activities, such as calling distinct categories of clients and prospects, training staff, working on financial projections, developing proposals or presentations, networking, etc. Also list your volunteer activities, personal care routines, personal development, leisure, and so on.

As you rate your involvements, beware of the tendency to yield to the status quo. Be brutally honest with yourself and deeply respectful of your vision and values.

Then, for each involvement, add across categories to get a total value. Compare the range of values. What do they reveal? Are there any surprises?

As you look at the results, also consider the possibility that some of your activities may be redundant. For example, you may love the arts and spend leisure time playing piano and guitar, painting and attending poetry readings. While all of these are enjoyable, focusing on one or two creative outlets may be equally fulfilling and, perhaps, even more enjoyable by virtue of greater focus.

a) A goal to focus on is to reduce, delegate, or eliminate half of your involvements and upgrade your efficiency by using creative solutions that yield greater results with less effort. This leads to enhancing your top priorities and opening you up to new opportunities (that's where the income double comes in!).

b) Making changes based on the Involvements Inventory can be life-altering! Complete the exercise with your full level of commitment: It may just be the one tool from this book that yields you the greatest benefit.

## REQUESTS / DEMANDS

Now let's think about how you tend to get pulled into too many involvements in the first place, and consider how to avoid this problem in the future. Chances are that you are someone who has a hard time saying "no" when it's clear that your time and energy are requested. It's time to learn different ways of dealing with requests for your involvement. Instead of believing that acceptance is the only right response to a request, consider the following choices you always have when someone makes a request of you:

1. Accept the request
2. Decline
3. Counteroffer
4. Defer

To accept is to simply say "yes." There are certainly times when that is the best choice and anything else would have significantly negative consequences. There will also be times when you are so certain that the request would be beneficial to you and/or the beneficiary of your time and energy. Say "yes" to sure things and best bets!

To decline is to simply say "no." Have you noticed that some people just say no and have no problem with that? Under what circumstances are you ready, willing, and able to say "no" instead of "yes" to a request?

To counteroffer is to offer an alternative. When someone makes a request that doesn't thrill you or does not fit with your commitments, you don't have to say "yes." Instead, you can say, "I'd love to say 'yes,' but here's what I *can* do instead." Then you can honor the person making the request by coming up with an alternative. For example, if someone asks you to volunteer for a function or cause that will take 2 hours a week for the next 10 weeks (20 hours), you could instead:

- Offer to split the involvement with someone if they agree to find someone else to share the responsibility. Time saved – 10 hours.
- Offer to spend 2 hours on the phone seeking someone else to take on the responsibility. Time saved 18 hours.
- Offer to spend a half hour talking about the responsibility and to provide a list of 5 names of other potential volunteers. Time saved: 19.5 hours.
- Suggest a website like Craigslist.com upon which they can post a request for volunteers. Time saved: 19 hours, 55 minutes!

This creates a win-win situation by virtue of expressing your willingness to help, while you remain in control of your time and avoid getting immersed in a new involvement. If you look back at your Involvements Inventory, can you identify times when you would have liked to have used this technique? Are there people currently making requests of you whom you'd like to try this with?

To defer is to simply ask for time before you make the decision. It sounds like this. "I'd like to say yes to you, but I need time to consider the request. Let me sleep on it, and I'll let you know tomorrow if I'll say yes or offer other alternatives." Can you see how giving yourself time to think could help you get out of a lot of unwanted situations? It is important for your reputation and integrity to respond on time with your answer, be it "yes," "no," or "here's what I *can* do."

I hired a coach to help me focus on growing my business. Although I was committed to my business, I also had several volunteer activities that I had agreed to. I was feeling very stretched and very stressed. Like many people, I volunteer for different organizations because their mission is meaningful to me. However, life changes, and even if an involvement satisfies one need, it may conflict with another that may be even more important. Also, we all can get burned out and get to the point where we are no longer as effective or committed and we have gone beyond our ability to contribute fully.

The "Involvements Inventory" exercise was really helpful to me because it forced me to take a snapshot of everything I do. I took a hard look and asked myself, "What am I doing, what needs and values does each involvement satisfy, and what would my life be like without it?"

Some responsibilities were not terribly time consuming, but each one was one more thing on my plate, and I felt that my effectiveness in every position was deteriorating. I was experiencing a lot of internal stress, both in terms of not being able to fully devote myself to my career and also not being able to give what I would have liked to in my volunteer positions.

Going through the exercise was terrific because it taught me to be mindful of the value of exiting gracefully and at the right time. However, we don't always know the right way to say goodbye and move on. I had some difficult conversations and made the tough choice to exit a few of my over-involvements. It was very hard in some cases to give some things up because I did enjoy and bring value to these organizations. On the flip side, it was a great relief as it freed up time and mental space so I could more fully engage in the things that I'm committed to and be more effective all around. I am now more comfortable with saying no and turning things down. I am continually mindful of my commitments, their impact on one another, and my sense of balance." - With permission from Ann Tedesco

Over-involvement overloads you, overwhelms you, and can make you feel scattered. Isn't it time to stop that feeling like you're always straining to catch up? Choosing to eliminate the involvements that are not your very best bets allows you to move on and focus on inspiring, relevant choices that further your goals for a better life with less trouble. Even though it is hard to say goodbye, people will understand.

And the people who get a more dedicated and energized you will be more supportive of you getting more out of what you put in. In short, you'll provide more value and attract more income!

---

### Challenge Homework

1. Using the Involvements Inventory worksheet, cut 50% of your involvements that do not provide you with outstanding added value (personally or professionally) or the opportunity for you to provide outstanding value.
2. Make a short list of the kinds of requests people have made of you, and then write up counteroffers that could shift the burden off your shoulders using "no" and "here's what I can do." Then practice this method the next time someone makes a request of you.

---

# Chapter 8
# Relationship Energy Drains

*"The person who says it cannot be done must not interrupt the person already doing it."*

—*Chinese proverb.*

Is there anything we do to create income that doesn't involve other people? Very little. Even something as internal as your health requires you to interact with practitioners who will help you monitor and correct any obstacles to optimal wellness.

People make up a significant part of your environment. If you believe that by taking better care of your environment, your environment will take much better care of you, then the subject of relationships with people is one of the most important issues for you to address.

Sometimes we put up with people who drain us because we feel we are stuck with them. Often we don't speak up about things that bother us because we don't want to make someone else feel bad. Sometimes we just don't know how to be more assertive without being dismissive. We all want to be liked and don't want to rock the boat.

In this chapter, we will examine how some aspects of relationships interfere with your ideal path to success, and we will employ a tool and process for removing the trouble without necessarily eliminating any people from your life. While this chapter focuses on energy-draining people and negative aspects of relationships, Chapter 14 is dedicated to building strong relationships with the ideal kind of people you can interact with in your life.

I'm sure we'd all agree that it is important to not let other people's negative energy bring you down. In the 2008 Broadway revival of *South Pacific*, Nelly sings, "I'm gonna wash that man right out of my hair, and send him on his way." While sometimes that might be the right thing to do, for now we will consider that step a last resort. Sometimes you can re-educate a person to treat you differently, and that is a valuable process if the person is important to you, like your spouse, close friend, coworker, or an important client.

The process of remodeling a relationship to eliminate its energy-draining aspects requires a healthy dose of self-respect and courage. You may need to reflect on your beliefs as to what you deserve and affirm that you are worthy of ideal treatment and interactions. If you need a bit of support on your sense of self-worth and empowerment, refer back to the Frame-Shifting-Frame in Chapter 3 and recall or explore new empowering beliefs to guide your new life.

By putting up with negative relationships, you are training people around you to continue to treat you that way. What can you do about people with whom you deal on a regular basis who repeatedly behave in a way that is draining or uninspiring to you? To retrain them, you need to establish proper boundaries.

We've all heard the saying "Good fences make good neighbors." Setting up boundaries is not about building impenetrable walls to keep people away from you. Good boundaries are best when they limit or eliminate specific behaviors or communication so you *can* allow people to get close to you without getting hurt or drained yourself. A large dose of compassion, patience, and respect—especially self-respect—are valuable in establishing and maintaining boundaries.

Here is a step-by-step approach with a bold exemplary scenario.[2]* Suppose you are working with an assistant who frequently barges into your office and interrupts you. You've decided you no longer want to be interrupted when your door is closed, and you begin to tell him to understand that unless an issue is urgent, he must wait one hour or write you a note.

---

2 This concept is derived from ideas I remember from reading *Coach Yourself to Success : 101 Tips from a Personal Coach for Reaching Your Goals at Work and in Life* by Talane Miedaner

## STEP 1: NOTIFY

First, make an initial, overall declaration that you will not tolerate or interact with the specific behavior. You may want to start with an overall declaration like, "You know how sometimes you come into my office when I'm focused on something else? I need to tell you that doing so is not an effective way to get my attention and, with all due respect, that doesn't work for me anymore. From now on, I will be making you aware if it by raising my hand like a stop sign, with no disrespect intended, so you can begin to practice gathering your questions for when I have a break in my focus." It is important, when making such a declaration, that you present a positive alternative.

The other part of this first step of informing occurs whenever (or if ever) the person exhibits the behavior. If your assistant forgets and barges in, you politely let him know that it's happening in the moment. You simply raise your hand and say, "Excuse me, you are interrupting me. As I told you I would, I am simply and respectfully pointing it out. My attention is focused on other things right now."

It is important that in each of these steps you use a nonjudgmental, neutral tone of voice, one that is calm, informative, and collaborative. Always understand that people may not intend to be any trouble. Understanding this thoroughly will help you avoid the temptation to present boundaries with anger or blame, which could cause the other person to get defensive. Make sure that your compassion is sincerely received.

## STEP 2: RE-DIRECT

If your assistant continues the habit after you have informed him on the spot, ask him politely to stop and request that he refrain from interrupting you unless it is timely and urgent. It is helpful to phrase your request directly in terms of what you *do* want, instead of what you don't want. For example, "Please come back at 1:00 when I will take a break and respond to all non-urgent matters."

## STEP 3: IMPLORE

If the notification and a simple request don't work, then go to the next level, but remain respectful while also maintaining self-respect. I choose the word implore because it is a more earnest version of a request. Sometimes you have to get eye-to-eye with someone and let them know that your request is serious and important to you. It is important to not be critical or harsh to the person you're speaking to – in fact, a dose of vulnerability could go a long way. But you must be sure that your request is taken seriously and understood on a deeper level. For example, "Joe, I really need to clarify, heart to heart, that I need you to stop interrupting me as often as you do. I believe you want your communication to be effective, but these intrusions are *not* effective. For our mutual benefit, I insist that you use our system – I'll be available at 1:00."

## STEP 4: LEVERAGE A CONSEQUENCE OR REWARD

If imploring doesn't work—because the person either just doesn't get that this is important to you or because he or she can't quit the bad habit—then you have to try giving the person a bit more motivation. That involves specifying a consequence or reward. To carry through with our example, "I must let you know now that after having asked a few times for you to stop interrupting, I am personally not able to tolerate the habit any more. If you don't stop, I will (take away a privilege, remove a convenience, or even begin disciplinary process that could lead to getting fired). Whatever consequence you suggest, make sure it is fair and reasonable and make sure it is something you would carry out. Also make sure the consequence doesn't punish you as well! That is why it can be much better to offer a reward. For example, "Joe, over the next 2 months, I'll treat you to lunch on Friday if we go a whole week using our system for keeping the interruptions to a minimum. How would that sound to you?"

## STEP 5: FOLLOW THROUGH

If the person does not respond to the offer of a consequence, you must honor your own integrity and self-respect and enact the consequence. If you offer a consequence but don't enforce it, you may never be taken seriously again. Then, if necessary, repeat these steps, but try to have a heart-to-heart talk before the behavior arises again.

Up until now, you have educated the people in your life about what kind of behavior is acceptable to you. Has the time come for you to firmly but respectfully re-educate people of your new standards? What might be possible if you had a few conversations for this level of consideration? What kind of treatment are you ready to eliminate from your life?

| NAME | RELATIONSHIP | BEHAVIOR |
|------|--------------|----------|
| 1. | | |
| 2. | | |
| 3. | | |
| 4. | | |

It may take a lot of courage to re-educate people as to what you're willing to put up with and what you are not, but your courage may lead to great confidence, respect, and empowerment, and it may help keep trouble far away from you.

### Challenge Homework

Make a list of people whose behavior is unacceptable and communicate your boundaries using the five-step model. Can you eliminate all or at least half the energy-draining interactions you otherwise put up with?

# Chapter 9
# High Standards – Nothing but the Best

*Somehow I can't believe that there are any heights that can't be scaled by a man who knows the secrets of making dreams come true. This special secret - curiosity, confidence, courage, and constancy, and the greatest of all is confidence. When you believe in a thing, believe in it all the way, implicitly and unquestionable. Do anything better than it was ever done before and you'll get rich."*

*- Walt Disney, entrepreneur*

It takes courage to reduce or eliminate obstacles in your life. Nevertheless, courage builds confidence while also making it possible to produce outstanding results. Another level of courage will be necessary for reducing or eliminating the next level of interference. This next level involves *raising your standards.*

Think about your standards. Do you put up with partners, clients, employees, or vendors who are "pretty good" but not great? Is your environment ideally and exceptionally suited to help you achieve your goals? What if you were to diligently require everything you allowed into your world to meet a level of quality that serves you nearly perfectly?

Do you have a pretty good accountant who is doing the job, but not talking to you about how to grow your business? Is she referring all her clients to you and vice-versa? Life is too short, and you need all your energy for making your life truly great. It's time to clear out not just the garbage in your life, but the whole bottom 80% to make plenty of room for the very best: the Top 20%.

For example, revisit the Involvements Inventory chart that you used in Chapter 8, where you created a list of your activities and ranked them from -10 to +10 in terms of emotional gain, financial cost, difficulty, etc. This sort of analysis helps you sort out which things are worth keeping in your life and which would make sense to let go of to free up valuable time and energy. On your first pass, you may have gotten rid of energy draining, low-level activities. Now you can refocus and reprioritize, limit, or eliminate activities that are OKAY and even GOOD, to make room for OUTSTANDING!

## WORKING WITH THE BEST, AND *ONLY* THE BEST

It's now time to apply the very highest standards to your relationships. Are you holding yourself back from being surrounded by outstanding people because the pretty good crowd has gotten comfortable?

Do you have clients who give you work that is not aligned to what you do best? Do you have clients who don't pay you what you know you're worth, but you keep them because you feel it's better to have the certain income rather than take a chance on not finding a replacement client? Isn't it time to stop thinking this way?

I believe that most people have a natural tendency to create and attract great things, unless there is interference. I have so often been amazed when I have witnessed the people I coach delete obstacles and interference, even when they seem to have it "good."

Like water breaking through a dam, they naturally gush forward with incredible energy, creating new pathways for success. It is exciting to watch!

This strategy of adopting the highest standards worked like a charm for one of my clients, an independent public relations specialist. She made a conscious decision to go from good to great in all aspects of her work. She changed the way she spoke about what she did, emphasizing being the best and working only with the most visionary and ambitious companies. She stopped giving potential clients the option to start at a low introductory rate because she found that once they started low, it was very hard to ever get them back to her ideal fee. She got up the courage to actually fire clients who didn't share her vision because they took up too much time and energy and prevented her from growing her business the way she wanted. But her income didn't suffer. As it turned out, her new way of presenting her services attracted lots of new clients who were of a higher caliber, even in the most dire economic environment (Fall 2008). Once she started attracting great clients who paid her what she was worth, she was able to hire great people to help her get the work done and free up her time to look for more great clients. She later announced that her income tripled as a result!

It is hard to let go of things that are "pretty good." But to the extent that you hang on to anything from the bottom 80%, you make less time and space available for the new "Top 20%" opportunities to occur or be duplicated. Conversely, the more you confidently clear the bottom 80% from your environment and involvements, the more that confidence, time, and space will be available to leverage your Top 20%. The enhancement and maintenance of high standards is an ongoing process that you can always improve.

If you maintain faith in yourself, your creativity and your resourcefulness, and if you keep building strong relationships with people who can contribute toward your most ideal vision, you will replace the energy drains, obstacles, and even some pretty good involvements with great, rewarding commitments that will yield extraordinary results.

## Challenge Homework

Review each of the chapters in Part II, and take it up a notch. For example, when you removed energy drains, you probably got rid of some junk from your closet. Now, go back to your closet and get rid of more of that stuff that doesn't serve you extraordinarily well and make you look and feel like a million bucks. Cut out everything in your life that isn't great—like the time you waste watching television shows that don't thrill you but you watch them simply because you have nothing better to do. Take inventory of everything you do and cut 50% or more of your troubles from your life. It will help you free up the time and energy you'll need for the next phase of this program.

# Part III
## Duplicate with Leverage

The first two parts of the book have hopefully enabled you to prepare the ground for a big step forward in doubling what comes into your life, and much of that preparation involves increasing the efficiency with which you are able to earn a living. You want to earn more while working less, but working better. In order to do that, you need to have created the right mental climate and also the right work environment, free of distractions and hassles.

If you have now attained that optimal environment, both inside and outside of your head, you are ready to really begin in earnest the process of leveraging your resources to duplicate your best successes. If you duplicate and leverage your best bets and follow through with confidence, you can DO LESS with ease and ATTRACT more – TWICE AS MUCH more!

I truly believe that all human beings are infinitely creative and resourceful and, when unblocked, naturally tend to attract the very best life has to offer. I have based most of my work on this premise, and my experience has shown that when people eliminate obstacles, they discover their greatness and put it to use. Of course, the challenge is identifying and removing the blocks and obstacles, which is a big part of what I do in coaching. If you have been removing blocks and energy drains with the help of the exercises in the preceding chapters, you should be finding by now that you are already attracting at least some of what you want to "come in" to your life.

If it's not working out that way for you, consider the following possibilities:

- **Your beliefs may not be aligned with your goals.** You might be going through the motions of this process, hoping this book will "do it" *for* you. It won't. You need to believe from the bottom of your heart that you are connected to the infinite source of possibilities and take actions consistent with that belief. Review the Frame-Shifting exercise in Chapter 2 and make sure you have cleared out limiting beliefs, particularly if there is a big one holding you back. Better yet, schedule a few sessions with me or the coach of your choice to make sure you are not missing any blind spots. The investment of time and money will be negligible compared to what will be possible if you are committed to having your income double with half the trouble.

- **You may not be adequately working through all the steps.** If you have shortchanged yourself, take time NOW to catch up and do the challenging exercise that you skipped or did in a half-assed manner. If these exercises are hard for you, welcome to boot camp! Remember that difficult things almost always get easier with practice. (Think of your own experiences working out, swimming, riding a bicycle, learning how to make sales calls, or using other business skills that were hard at first, and how with time you developed strength that made these skills a breeze for you).

Be patient and keep going. Believe in possibilities that you will succeed and stay focused and committed to trying new things and learning. Don't be afraid to reach out for help along the way. You can't fail if you don't give up!

Now that you have a newly cleared foundation, the next steps involve figuring out how to duplicate what you do best and begin leveraging your assets to get more income with less time spent. You've cleared out as much as possible from the bottom 80% of your life, and you should have much more time, space, and mental bandwidth at your disposal for duplicating the top 20% of your resources that have yielded the top 80% of your income.

To start duplicating, you first need to do two things:

1. Identify your best bets, or your Top 20%, as I like to call it, and then...
2. Focus your time, energy, and resources to pursue that Top 20% in order to duplicate it.

The first chapter in this section will deepen your understanding of leverage and show you how to identify your Top 20% and make plans to duplicate it. Chapter 11 (perhaps ironically) focuses on leveraging and doubling the value you provide professionally, which is tied to how you price your services and earn money. Chapter 12 builds on the importance of relationships and how to add some new, influential people to your team, so you have a network of people to help you duplicate your best bets. Then Chapter 13 will help you put in all together with systems and structures, including an approach to time management, that will enable you to enact your plans and stay focused on your goals.

Enjoy the ride!

# Chapter 10

# Leverage

*"Just as the hand, held before the eye, can hide the tallest mountain, so the routine of everyday life can keep us from seeing the vast radiance and the secret wonders that fill the world."*
*-18th century Chasidic saying.*

Leverage is the process of creating multiple positive outcomes from any given input. Whenever you use a bottle opener to remove a bottle top with an easy flick of the wrist—something your fingers alone couldn't do, regardless of your strength—that's leverage.

If you swim with fins, you know that sense of powerful forward propulsion you get with the slightest flutter of your legs. That's leverage.

If you ever send out mass emailings, you experience how computer software design enables you to reach many people instantaneously, whereas regular mail or other means of communication takes much more time. That's leverage.

Machines provide leverage. Design provides leverage. Communication provides leverage.

Let me give you a simple example from my own experience. In 2004, I committed myself to having an impact in the presidential election. My first approach was to get more voters registered in the swing state of Pennsylvania. I traveled for five hours to reach voters in Lancaster, walked door-to-door for about eight hours, and then drove home. That 18-hour day resulted in six new voters registered. While that counts as leverage because I added six potential voters to my lone vote, it felt like a ridiculously small result for the 18-hour investment. I thought there had to be a better way.

Considering that my own personal strengths include coaching, training, transferring enthusiasm (motivating), and using the telephone, I found a website that directed me to call people who were looking to volunteer like I had. I sat down for two hours and spoke with ten people, instructing them and motivating them to make a day of door-to-door registrations like I had. By conservative estimates, if only eight of those ten people followed through and were able to register only half the number of people I had (six), then I had influenced 24 voters with that effort. Let's compare:

Plan A: 6 votes in 18 hours (3 hours of my time per vote)

Plan B: 24 votes in 2 hours (12 votes per hour of my time)

Then in 2008, I sharpened the saw even more. On two evenings in October, I turned my home into a call center, inviting and instructing more than ten friends and neighbors to phone volunteers (provided by MoveOn.org) in key battleground states. We reached and motivated approximately 75 volunteers who made a commitment to "get out the vote" in their neighborhood on a particular date and time. If only 80% of them, or 60 people, honored that commitment, and if each of them influenced 3 voters, we now have:

Plan C: 180 votes in 6 hours (30 votes per hour of my time)

See what I mean by leverage? Can you see how valuable this kind of thinking can be in making your own income double with half the trouble?

Some people ask me if leverage, as I use the word in this program, is the same thing as efficiency. I consider efficiency a cousin of what we're talking about—improvements in efficiency are good, but I want you to consider the kind of leverage that goes beyond incremental increases in output. We're looking for multiples of the outcome with simple, clever adjustments.

We're talking about breakthroughs!

Leverage involves exploring beyond working with what you know and going with what really works wonders! Most importantly, leverage involves knowing the right way to involve people and building a team of people with influence and leverage of their own.

A great example of leverage was on the reality television show, *The Apprentice*. During a semi-final episode, Kendra, the underdog, was teamed up with Craig, with whom she'd had much friction over the course of the show's competitions. Another contestant, Tana, was the favorite to win, as she had shown exceptional leadership all season long. She was paired up in this semi-final contest with Alex, a shrewd attorney. It seemed likely that Alex and Tana would win this contest selling t-shirts to be designed by a popular artist. But before long, Tana got caught up in a personal fascination with a design detail in the production of their product. She insisted on spending time trying to find and put to use a trendy device called the Bedazzler and convinced the pop-artist assigned to her team to use it in the creation of the t-shirts.

Meanwhile, Kendra put the concept of leverage into action. Instead of micro-managing the successful pop-artist's creative process, she focused on sales—the deciding factor in the contest. Rather than trying to sell the product one walk-in customer at a time, Kendra asked the artist a simple question: "Can we invite people from your mailing list to come visit the store and see the t-shirts?" The answer was yes. It was a stroke of genius. As a result of one simple mass e-mailing, the pop artist's fan base flocked to the store and paid top dollar for the limited edition t-shirt.

Previously, most other *Apprentice* contests had been decided by a 10% to 15% margin, at most. Kendra's savvy idea to leverage one key relationship was the factor that led her team to win the contest by 300%! Kendra went on to take top honors, and that season she became Donald Trump's apprentice.

At this point, you are most likely wondering, "How do I apply this concept in practical terms to my own situation? I'm already working as hard and as efficiently as I can!" That may seem true to you, so let's take a step back and gain perspective on how to identify and leverage your Top 20%.

## IDENTIFYING YOUR TOP 20%

As we have previously demonstrated, by clearing out obstacles and finding the 20% of your choices that yield 80% of your income, you can simply duplicate that one and half times ($80\% \times 2.5 = 200\%$) and only have to put in half the effort ($20\% \times 2.5 = 50\%$)

So what is your Top 20%? Think about your greatest successes and what resources, people, or ideas and ways of thinking were involved. Your greatest successes were based on certain opportunities that presented themselves and decisions that you made. How did these opportunities arise? Did something just fall into your lap or did it arise from actions you took? Most likely there were elements of both luck and action. What did you do to prepare the ground for a lucky situation to come about?

For example, I have a client who busied himself with a wide array of marketing methods to promote his executive recruiting services. He wrote and tried to publish articles, did a lot of networking, used direct mail, made follow-up sales calls, and, for a period of time, made public appearances on how to recruit executive talent. He explained why he wasn't consistent with the speaking engagements. "I used to love doing the events, but they were hardly worth it. Preparations are time-consuming, and I would only get one new client per event."

I was a little curious about his conflicting feelings, but it got more interesting when we explored which of his marketing activities attracted the most clients and which of his strategies attracted his very best clients. He met his best clients at conferences and seminars where he was perceived to be an expert by being at the front of the room. These events were filled with human resource executives from large corporations with the right projects and healthy recruiting budgets.

A few adjustments needed to be made to leverage this situation. We streamlined and automated the otherwise time-consuming preparation process. He also started to allow himself to enjoy these activities again, which made him more attractive to new clients during his presentations. He cut back on other activities so he could focus on booking twice as many speaking engagements. Since he was more engaged and engaging in the process, he doubled his revenue in one year.

It's easy to break down clients into categories of most valuable and least valuable and identify a Top 20%. Take a list of all of your clients over the last three to five years, and isolate your Top 20. Turn the information into a chart, like the one below.

## Top 20 Clients

| Name | Why they are in the Top 20 | How did you find them? |
|------|---------------------------|------------------------|
| 1 | | |
| 2 | | |
| 3 | | |
| 4 | | |
| 5 | | |
| 6 | | |
| 7 | | |
| 8 | | |
| 9 | | |
| .... | | |
| | | |
| 18 | | |
| 19 | | |
| 20 | | |
| | | |

You should be able to identify some sort of pattern or simply find that one or two of your best clients came to you in a similar way.

Then try to duplicate this result by putting more time and energy into doing whatever you did to attract your best clients.

For example, I worked with an orthodontist who had two offices. One was on the outskirts of a highly affluent community, and the other was in the midst of a working class community. Of course, his rent at the latter was about half of his rent at the former, so he thought he had a good deal going. He spent equal time at both offices and found considerable competition in both markets. When we started working together, he was afraid of putting all his eggs in one basket. Together we discovered that he much preferred working in the more affluent community where, by the way, he had a number of connections through friends and family. After a bit of frame-shifting in his own mind, he decided to go for it and relocated to an office smack dab in the middle of the more affluent neighborhood. He was introduced to many people and invited to many social functions. He donated gift certificates to local charity auctions as a way to quickly build awareness in the community of his expertise and character. He is well on his way to doubling his income and has also doubled his enjoyment, now that he wakes up every day to go to work in a community where he is known and loved. He cut his trouble in half by not having to run around between districts!

This may sound like it was a no-brainer. But typically, people go about their business hour-by-hour, day-by-day, and often don't stop to look at the larger picture. And it takes a certain amount of self-awareness and self-discipline to stay on track and stick to a plan that keeps you focused on your ideal client. Creating an ideal client profile can be a useful tool to help you succeed in the process.

## Profiling is Good!

Once you analyze your business and identify the clients who were involved in the greatest income-producing situations over, say, the last three years, you should next create profiles of the "right" kind of people to be the focus of your attention. By being very clear about the characteristics your best clients share, you will be in a better position to know how to find them. Try to quantify their traits as much as possible with precise numbers.

If your clients tend to be individuals, the elements of your profile might include the following details. You can create a document right away that describes your ideal clients based on criteria such as:

- Age (e.g., 30-50) _____
- Gender _____
- Marital status / family size (e.g., married with kids)
  _____
- Income (e.g., salary of at least $300,000)
  _____
- Geographic location / urban vs. suburban
  _____
- Favorite magazines (if relevant to your business)
  _____,
  _____,
  _____,
  _____,
  _____.

If your clients are companies, then the elements of your profile might include:

- Size (e.g., more than 100 employees)
  _____
- Field (e.g., creative, such as graphic design or advertising) _____
- Revenue (e.g., more than $10 million a year)
  _____
- Management style (less rigid, less hierarchical)
  _____

These are just some examples to get you thinking. The important thing is to determine which characteristics seem to impact your particular business. You may be able to identify those things on your own, or you may find it is worth while to hire a coach or a marketing consultant to help you.

It's a good idea to put your profile in writing, for two reasons:

- A visual representation of your requirements or preferences helps make these things better organized in your mind.
- A written version of your ideal client, edited as necessary, can be shared with other people to increase the chances of finding what you're looking for.

What other details would you use to describe your ideal client?

_____

_____

_____

_____

## DUPLICATING YOUR TOP 20%

Now that you have your profile for your ideal client, it is a simple matter of using the profile to come up with a list of clients you want to go after and then being persistent with marketing calls, networking, and devising creative ways of getting their attention, taking clues from how you attracted similar clients in the past. It also doesn't hurt to take some of your best clients to dinner and ask them for introductions and referrals.

I have a client who buys and sells rare art. For many years he fell short of his potential, because he would work with anyone regardless of the size of the deal or the buying potential of the client. His best clients bought and sold items worth millions of dollars, on which he would make a healthy commission. His lesser clients bought and sold items worth as little as a few thousand dollars and therefore each transaction yielded much lower earnings for a similar amount of work as the big deals. One of his challenges was that he was too busy running around taking care of all kinds of small projects. When we first analyzed revenue, 80% of his income came from eight big deals, while the remaining 20% came from about 30 or 40 smaller sales.

Together, we figured out how many million dollar deals he needed in order to eventually double his income.

By eliminating or vastly reducing those smaller, albeit interesting projects, he was better able to focus on his best clients. He started making time to get to know each of them better, strengthened his bonds with them and increased their trust in him. Perhaps even more importantly, the more regular communication with his most affluent clients allowed him to gain new insights on exactly what and when they wanted to buy or sell. In our first year working together, he was able to put together more focused, customized offerings for his best clients and, as a result, easily increased sale *and profit* by 20%. He was even able to move a significant, rare work (one of his best deals for the year) in late 2008 while the rest of the world was suffering from the stock market crash and economic turmoil.

So, now that you know the secret of leveraging, it's time to get to work analyzing your business, creating your own ideal client profiles, and taking action to go after what you want. One of my favorite quotes comes from Ken Blanchard, leadership guru and author of many best-selling business books. At a lecture a few years ago, he said, "Shoot for the bull's-eye – you may hit it! But if you shoot for the bull's-eye and miss, you are still on target. Most people shoot for the target called 'just getting by' or 'hanging in there.' If you shoot for *that* target and miss, you'll end up nowhere!" Therefore, I encourage you to always target your ideal clients, even if you sometimes think, "I don't know HOW the heck I WILL find them, but I believe that I CAN!" That kind of faith in the face of fear can put you into a creative state that inspires you to figure it out and make it happen.

Consider how, where, and with whom you have experienced your most significant victories, personal or professional. Use drawings, charts, photos, and cut-outs from magazines, create visual depictions to help you "see" your ideal profile come to life. And while you're thinking big, revamp your goals in all areas of your life to be aiming for the bull's-eye rather than just trying to get by.

---

**Challenge Homework**

1. Analyze your business and determine what constitutes your Top 20%.
2. Create a profile of your ideal client using relevant criteria, such as age, gender, family situation, income, location, etc. Put your profile in writing and post it where you can see it.
3. Set up a plan for taking the steps you need to take in order to duplicate your Top 20%. What calls do you need to make? What letters or e-mails do you need to write? What events or meetings do you need to attend? Make a list and set deadlines for accomplishing goals

---

# Chapter 11
# Value and Pricing

*"Show me the money!"*
*— Rod Tidwell, the character played by*
*Cuba Gooding Jr. in Jerry McGuire*

With a bolder goal, higher standards, and clearer profile for attracting your best clients; we can now talk about earning as much as possible by providing outstanding value for these people. Your goal is to not only charge a high price for your services but to also be worth that price. We're talking here about money and what makes you worth a lot of it to your clients. The first part of this discussion may bring us back to some of the limiting beliefs we explored in Part 1. It's important to realize that people have a psychological relationship with money, and attitudes toward the green stuff can sometimes be unhealthy or unbalanced. There is typically either too much focus on money or not enough.

Creating a healthy, balanced relationship with money is actually one of the most important tasks you can do both personally and professionally. Focusing too much on money itself, rather than on providing extraordinary value to your clients, is like watering the fruit on the tree rather than its roots. What would happen to the tree if you didn't nourish the base? The base of the tree for you is your quality of service, integrity, pride in your work, and professionalism.

Perhaps the extreme example of someone who focused too much on money is the disgraced investment guru Bernie Madoff, who bilked his clients of billions of dollars in one of grandest Ponzi schemes ever devised until it all fell apart at the end of 2008. Now, here was a man who focused on the fruit and let the tree completely wither away. As of this writing, he is (hopefully) going to jail. People who have an obsessive relationship with money and material things are consumed with that need. The focus is misplaced as these people miss opportunities to understand and meet or exceed the expectations of service and quality that customers respond to (with money).

One day, I walked into a music store and told the salesperson who greeted me that I was looking for a new electric piano and keyboard. The first question he asked me was, "How much are you looking to spend?" I was immediately turned off by his tone and did not give him my business. At the next music store, the salesman asked me what kind of music I play, what I wanted to use the keyboard for, and then what price range I was comfortable with. Big difference. The second salesman "got" that his role was not just about taking my money, but also about guiding me toward the right value for my money. Part and parcel of this value orientation are the notions of integrity and integration. If you feel great about the service you know you are providing, you will more confidently and more sincerely be able to attract business and perhaps even quote higher prices that reflect that value.

Of course, ignoring money matters is not the answer, either. Being unbalanced about money can show up when a business person cares too deeply and passionately about helping others, without a healthy ability to monetize the value of what he or she provides. Such folks end up drained and burnt out and sometimes broke. A graphic artist client I worked with in New York City, when given an assignment to draft ideas for his clients, would regularly work on and present over 30 different options, when really only three to five were expected. This took so much of his time that he was not able to serve enough clients to make a decent living. But he didn't charge a cent more for doing ten times the work. When I asked him why he did it, he said, "I just love giving my clients a lot to choose from, and I think they have come to expect this level of service." (It turns out that when he asked his clients about this, they actually preferred fewer choices, as too many options made the decision process too difficult.)

For a balanced relationship with money, appreciate and honor its importance and charge what the value you provide is truly worth, but keep yourself focused on providing the value. Here's how:

## PRICING

This is one of my favorite areas to coach people, because I so frequently find people undercharging and selling themselves short, and it is very rewarding (and provides my clients an excellent return on investment) when I can help them increase income and also gain greater respect by pricing goods or services more accurately.

Pricing is influenced by several factors.

- **The competitive marketplace.** What are others charging? What will the market bear? Gasoline prices are a commodity set very competitively, with some gas stations simply making a practice of beating the competition down the street by one or two cents. Competitors to consider are not only the direct competitors, but indirect solutions as well. When considering transportation to the airport, we don't consider only the cost of one livery service versus another, we also consider the cost (in time and money) involved in taking the train or bus or driving and parking ourselves.
- **The real and perceived value of your unique service.** How badly does the customer want your stuff over anyone else's? And how much more value does your solution provide than other solutions? A private driver costs more than the bus for obvious reasons. Is Starbuck's coffee really twice as good as Dunkin' Donut's coffee at half the price? (It's debatable, I'm told – I'm not really a coffee drinker.)
- **Guts.** Your willingness to boldly set your prices as high as possible is the filter for the other two factors. If you don't believe in your value as compared to the competition, or in the eyes and emotions of your target market, you may not price your work accurately.

Therefore, pricing requires some research about your competitors' pricing and awareness of what people spend to alleviate the pain or need that you serve. If you haven't yet done so, go find out what your top 10 competitors charge. It is important to know why the low-cost provider is cheaper and why the premium provider commands a higher price. For example, Apple's Mac computers are priced higher than comparable PCs for many reasons. The level of design, virus immunity, and service go far and above what other computer manufactures offer. They also offer simplicity of choices, which makes the buying experience completely stress free.

I recently met a partner in a dental practice in Connecticut that practices a philosophy of "WOWing patients AND each other" on a daily basis. If someone comes in for a cleaning on her birthday, she gets a cake! If a patient or someone the patient knows has a baby, the new mother gets a complete pediatric dental gift basket. They have video games for kids to play in the waiting room. This practice not only is the largest dental practice I've ever heard of (over 100 employees), but they also get paid in full by their patients – they do not accept payment from third-party dental insurance plans.

It is critical to know how your product/services can be better or more valuable than anyone else's. If you're going to charge more, consider how you will be perceived as providing greater quality or value. How will you build up your reputation to enhance the perception of your value? I will again recommend that you brainstorm or survey your customers or potential customers to get some answers. It is an exciting conversation to have from time to time.

Once you have a sense of the competitive marketplace and the perceived value you provide, how do you come up with a number?

In order to arrive at the right price points, I like to think in terms of five possible facial expressions that correspond to clients' reactions to price quotes, or The 5 Faces of Negotiation (see Figure 5).

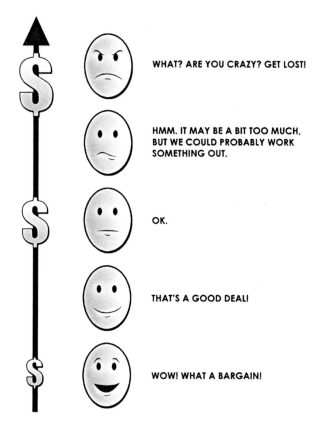

**Figure 5** The 5 Faces of Negotiation.

Look at the frowning face on the top of Figure 5. It represents the reaction you might elicit if you cross the price threshold beyond which your client will be angry or insulted. You don't want to start with a number that would make someone think you're just plain crazy and therefore not engage in negotiation. Think of the times that something has been way too expensive for you to even consider. You quickly dismiss the possibility of the transaction, right? You should avoid this price point unless you actually DON'T want to do business with that client or customer!

Now take a look at the bottom two faces. If the client's expression is either happy (second from the bottom) or ecstatic (the very bottom), then you are providing a bargain and starting with a happy client (a good thing) but probably putting less money in your pocket than you could. Sometimes, it is wise strategically to undercharge as either an enticing introduction to a business relationship or as a reward for a longstanding business relationship. Generosity can be attractive. However, undervaluing yourself as a habit does not garner respect, nor is it recognized as generosity. If you give someone a great deal, make sure in a subtle way that the person knows the true value of what you're offering and the amount of generosity you are providing. Otherwise, you may come across as having low self-worth and low self-esteem–and clients may get used to taking advantage of you and continuously demand more from you for less pay! Sometimes the lowest-paying clients give us the most headaches. When low-paying clients are taking up a lot of energy and attention, we can't give our highest-paying clients our best level of attention.

If you get a neutral, painless, "Okay, I'll take it," without any hesitation (the middle face), then you probably proposed a fair price. That has advantages as you are building relationships, and it doesn't hurt to shoot for this amount. However, as this topic is about maximizing your earnings, you leave something at the table when the person feels no pain at all in paying your fee.

The second face from the top, the one just underneath the frowning face, depicts the ideal client reaction—the one you really want to aim for to maximize your income. This client is a little troubled at first but is not going to walk away. This client will consider your offer and will either accept it or continue talking to you to get to a deal that is just at the threshold of what is acceptable to him. It may be a slightly lower price or it may be a little extra service. That is exactly where you want to be. You will then have a conversation that leads to a win-win situation. If you don't mind dealing with some resistance and handling some objections and issues up front with your client, then you should identify this amount to initiate any negotiation. If you have done some research or have good instincts, AND have the guts to ask for a nearly audacious price, you'll have a good idea of how much you can ask for without turning the other person away.

For example, my client Susan had started a consultancy built around her expertise with food allergies. She had launched a Web log that quickly got recognized by the *New York Times* and *The Wall Street Journal*. She had to come up with new ways to generate income, so we talked about how she was providing exposure and positive impressions for some of the companies that she wrote about on her blog. She considered inviting them to advertise on her website.

She agreed with the idea and got some information about how other bloggers charge advertisers. However, after a few weeks, she wasn't making the calls. She was afraid that the business owners would resent being asked for money after getting free publicity from Susan's blog. She had to shift away from a limiting belief that went something like, "If I ask for money, people will see me as mercenary and will be annoyed and hate me." Of course, in reality, there is plenty of evidence that people who exchange money can also have great affinity for each other—the two things are not mutually exclusive! It is important to find the right way to make your requests with sensitivity and appropriateness, taking into account the situation or issues a person might have with regard to the request you're making.

It was going to take some boldness on her part, but she made a big shift and made some big requests!

She recounted saying, "You like me, I like you, and when anyone types your company name into Google, I come up as number two. So why don't we capitalize on that? When people are reading about your company on my site, it makes sense to have an ad there, too."

"What was the response?" I asked.

"Both companies I asked to advertise were totally open to the conversation, a bit concerned at first when I told them my price, but we settled on a good rate and an annual commitment."

I asked Susan, "What was the big lesson for you?"

"Although these are relationships that I had been building for several months, I was still nervous making the call because I'm not always comfortable asking for a high price - I really had to build up the courage and go for it!"

"Did that exercise help you build confidence for future situations like that?" I asked.

"Yes. Sometimes you need a new kind of success, and you need a new pathway to that success. I tried something different, and now I have the confidence because I know it can work!"

So here is the lesson to take away from these silly drawings of faces: While it is only human that you would want to see neutral, happy, or ecstatic facial expressions on your clients, as a businessperson you need to realize that these are all indications that you've undercharged. Don't be afraid to get the slightly pained look that will lead to a successful negotiation and a good, but fair, price.

Finally, when considering pricing, you can get information about what clients are willing to pay by offering options. When you go the movies, you are always presented with a choice of small, medium, and large popcorn. Usually the smallest popcorn size is ridiculously small, thus leading people to order medium (most often) or large. The largest sizes are priced only a little more than the medium popcorn (only 50 cents, for example) but the cost to manufacture a slightly bigger bag and add a few ounces of popcorn can be pennies—thus, the movie theatre generates a nice extra profit. In a similar way, you can create "good," "better," and "best value" price points that guide your customers to a price that provides you with an excellent profit. In my own work as a business coach, for example, I offer private coaching with the maximum personal attention at my highest fee level. Clients who want the red carpet treatment and are pursuing a large enough goal for a windfall and a large return on investment opt for that level of service. At the mid-range, I put two clients together in a "Group-of Two" format. During the shared session, each client gets a half hour of dedicated attention, but semi-privately. Then they listen to the other client being coached, and sometimes give as well as receive added value from that part of the session. At the low end, I have coaching groups during which each client can report in and set goals every session, but will not be guaranteed dedicated attention in each session.

## Adding Value

As you progress in business, it is important for you to continually get better at these ways of making more money and to train the people around you to continually get better at it, too. The more your people can run and grow your business for you, the more you can reward them and also be on the lookout for new opportunities. With technology advancing at such a rapid pace and the economic and environmental issues shaking up global commerce, there are always new opportunities to find new ways to serve people's needs and run a profitable business. Always be open to new opportunities, especially as they fit your core expertise. For example, a wedding videographer created a podcast that brides-to-be can download and listen to in order to get information on all aspects of planning a wedding. He also provides a free, in-studio engagement video to every couple who books him to shoot their wedding. He finds that such a gift generates a tremendous amount of goodwill with his clients and gives them some immediate gratification in the face of a long process. It also significantly increases his exposure as the bride and grooms send the "YouTube Proposal" to friends and relatives, which leads to significantly more referrals.

People usually buy from people they know, like, and trust. If your customers already know you and trust you, these customers will be more receptive to your solutions to their needs than will new people you have never met before. Therefore, one of your best bets for increasing your success is to add value to what you already do for the people who already like and trust you.

Adding value can occur in any number of ways. Your challenge is to figure out how to do this in your business. I'm sure you ask, from time to time, "What else can I do for you?" When was the last time you asked a client to really engage in a conversation to dig deeper into that question? Wouldn't it be worth the time to figure out what your clients want and need, perhaps beyond what they even think or know that they need? This research about out how your clients deal with the challenges they face can uncover some terrific opportunities, as well as creating a stronger relationship with the clients you interview. Do a study of how you can blow the lid off how you provide value to your clients, and you'll find many of them wanting to pay you even more than you ever dreamed of charging them.

Finding new ways of serving your clients is easier said than done, but I invite you to trust that with your infinite creativity and resourcefulness, plus a willingness to collaborate with your customers, you can find brilliant solutions. The goal is to price your services so that as you add value or become more aware of the true value you provide, you can ask for and earn what you are truly worth.

## Brainstorming

With new input about what your clients want and need, the brainstorming process can help you explore ideas for delivering value that would never occur to you by yourself. It is always helpful to explore the infinite creativity and resourcefulness of the people around you, especially those who care about your well-being. Sometimes really simple but excellent ideas can come from other people's observations of how you run your business, even if they are not experts in your field. Plus, other people don't have the mental blind spots or fears that might be keeping you from your most powerful possibilities.

For example, another photographer who had been in business for over twenty-five years was given a simple suggestion by his brand-new employee, a young woman right out of school. She thought they should leave the door to the storefront open in the summertime so that people would feel freer to saunter in rather than having to ring the bell and wait for someone to let them in. The photographer had always operated on a "by appointment only" policy, but decided to try it, not expecting to see much of an effect. Lo and behold, once the door was left open, his walk-in business became a significant part of overall sales, increasing business by 50 percent. Somehow, the open-door policy made a big psychological difference for people. It took an outside observer to see that. And, fortunately for the photographer, she wasn't afraid to speak up.

One of the best ways to tap into new ideas is through organized brainstorming. The idea is to gather some of the most creative people you know, including clients if you can, and come up with ideas together for providing greater value.

Several years ago I worked for firm that consulted to major brands on how to license their logo and brand awareness. At the beginning of each assignment, we'd gather two dozen of our most creative friends and brainstorm about possible extensions for historic brands like Western Union®, Winchester®, Kodak®, and many others. One of the ideas we came up with was to lend the Kodak® brand to the Christmas tree lights industry. We found a manufacturer who was tired of constantly fighting the price war and ending up the second largest seller of Christmas tree lights. With the Kodak® brand and some quality enhancements, they were able to sell a premium product at a premium price.

You can get an extraordinary array of ideas by brainstorming with just a handful of big thinkers, with a particularly creative individual such as a mentor, advisor or coach, or you could create a "brainstorming party" to get the broadest and best ideas in an exciting forum.

Here are the steps to making the brainstorming process work best for you:

1. Invite a diverse array of people to be part of the process with you. If you only invite like-minded people or clones of yourself, you'll miss out on great ideas. Invite members of your target market, but also invite people who have very different ideas and experiences. Sometimes the best "out of the box" ideas come from people who really live outside of the box.

2. Make sure people know what they are coming to do. Plan to meet in a place where everyone can be comfortable and can write ideas down as they come up.

3. Make sure they all know to be on time. You want to conduct a brainstorming session without interruptions so the creative energy is focused and nurtured.

4. When people arrive, make sure they are comfortable with the environment and the situation. Ask them, "What can I do to make you comfortable?" Offer them food, drink, and a comfortable place to sit. Adjust the room temperature as necessary.

5. Make sure the brainstorming topic is clear. Provide adequate background information and clarify the question. For example, don't ask, "How can I make more money in my business?" Instead, brief people on how your clients, for example, business administrators at hospitals, need to have more tools to manage their time and the people around them, and ask "What are some ways we could add value to the time tracking software we distribute?"

6. Let everyone know that one person at a time should be speaking, and to jot down every idea they have or any idea they like, so if they don't get a chance to speak right away, they can still capture their idea and share it later.

7. Let everyone ask questions as necessary. However, encourage them not to let your answers limit the idea flow. Here's why.

8. Good ideas, weird ideas, bad ideas, practical and impractical ideas, off-the-wall ideas, and boring ideas are all IDEAS. And ideas lead to more ideas. And more ideas lead to new, breakthrough, innovative ideas. Let everyone know the number one rule is "NEVER NEGATE." Encourage anyone who is stuck on coming up with another idea to consider one of the worst ideas on the table and think of how to make it an extraordinary idea.

9. Use random triggers to get people thinking beyond the normal constraints. Take a random item in the room, a picture in a magazine, or someone's favorite food and ask, "What are the characteristics of this item?" Then ask, "How could we find an idea that also has those characteristics?" For example, I had a client who was stuck on how to deal with an overwhelming number of phone calls to return every day. As we were brainstorming, I asked her to come up with a random subject to stimulate our thinking. She cited a long-necked swan - a quiet and calm creature that doesn't let anything ruffle its feathers. Inspired by that seemingly random thought, she decided to "stick her neck out" and extend calmer, more graceful listening skills. She was then able to complete her calls much faster than before because she stopped interrupting and debating unnecessarily during each conversation.

10. As a way to lead to your wrap-up, end with a few "sprints." Invite the group to come up with 20 ideas in the next 5 minutes (or something like that). A strange thing about creativity is that creative people, when properly motivated, create more creative ideas when they are faced with greater constraints. A great example of this is depicted in the story of the *Apollo 13* mission, portrayed in a film starring Tom Hanks and Gary Senise. The ground crew has to figure out a way to retrofit a round air filter with a square housing, using the very few random materials found on the Lunar Module and landing capsule.

11. When everyone is done, thank them profusely and lead the group into a group cheer or dance. If people leave your brainstorming session feeling great about doing it, they are more likely to come back again when you need them. If appropriate, perhaps offer coupons or special offers related to your service as a thank-you gift to your attendees. The recipients can use the coupons or pass them on to other potential clients.

If you get a clear idea of what your customers desperately need or deeply desire, then you can come up with innovative ways to serve those needs better than it they are currently being served. Then you can offer more value at the right price, a higher price, and make more money while building an even stronger relationship with your clients!

---

### Challenge Homework

1. Do a study of how you can blow the lid off how you provide value to your clients. Ask clients to really dig deep for an answer that would make a huge difference.
2. Host a "brainstorming party" to create new ways of wowing your clients, and then offer to facilitate a brainstorming session on behalf of one of your participants.

---

# Chapter 12
## The Best People – Your People

*"Play the 'Reverse Gossip' Game. See how many nice things you can say behind someone's back."*
*- Bob Burg, bestselling author/speaker/networking guru*

Just last week, a client of mine introduced me to a collector of rare historic documents from the late 18th and 19th centuries. As we were getting to know each other, he asked me, "What do you collect?"

Without much thought, I answered, "Nothing, really."

However, the question got me thinking. Collectors have a passion for a subject and spend time and money building, sharing, and enjoying their collection of rarities. They get energized just thinking about the favorites in their collection and about making new discoveries. I remember when I was growing up, my piano teacher had a brilliant collection of over 100 miniature sculpted owls. My mother collects miniature pianos and proudly displays them near her concert grand piano. A former coworker of mine has a huge and valuable collection of historic Disney character toys and merchandise.

I may not collect anything miniature or historic, but I realized as I was driving home that evening that my answer to the coin and document dealer was inaccurate. It may sound a little strange, but I'm a passionate collector of great relationships with extraordinary people. Just like the most avid collectors I've known, I spend a significant majority of my time adding to, enhancing, enjoying and sharing favorites in my collection and I always get excited about new discoveries. It may sound like an unusual collection, but I really do enjoy making new contacts and building relationships with progressive, adventurous souls who have great ambition and a commitment to make

119

a difference in the world. I <u>love</u> learning about what people do and what trouble they struggle with and what their strengths are and where they get stuck and what helps them move them forward and how they navigate and celebrate the ups and downs in life. Like a collector of rare historic documents, I treat almost everyone I meet with great respect and awe – because *every one* is precious. The point of telling you all this is really to introduce the idea that everyone actually has some collection of relationships and stepping up how you care for this aspect of your life and your business is critical for happiness and success.

Research has proven time and again that business success and personal happiness are based mostly on the quality of relationships we manage. So in a way, I could consider myself lucky to have focused on this kind of collection - extraordinary relationships with people.

There is an endless supply of books on the subject of relationships, so rather than try to be too comprehensive here, I will focus on what I have found to be the three most important aspects of relationships as they relate to attracting what you want to have "come in" to your life with greatest ease:

1. Surrounding yourself with a "team" of your ideal people to extend your reach toward the life you want and truly deserve.
2. Building strong foundations in relationships.
3. Making bold requests and being persistent yet respectful.

## Gathering a Team

One of the best ways to help support your pursuits is to have a team around you willing to challenge you and hold you to your extraordinary commitment. A team doesn't have to be an organized group or hired employees: Your team can be a set of individuals in your life that you designate to talk with you about your approach to the bold concepts in this book (with or without referring to the book itself!) A team can be a group of friends that hangs out together or a list of friends that you spend time with individually. (It's loads of fun to put them together if they are not already organized in a group.)

If you did the exercises in Part 2 and got rid of—or built better boundaries with—people who drain your energy, you can focus on gathering people who are living bold, exciting lives (or are willing to start), similar to the one you are currently in the process of building.

How and where do you find them?

It doesn't happen overnight. In fact, it is a lifelong work-in-progress! However, you can gain momentum by attending business network groups, meet-up groups, seminars, workshops, and/or volunteer events that are meaningful to you. You could cultivate a hobby or take that course you've always wanted to take. You are sure to meet like-minded people if you follow where your mind and heart lead you. Such networking is a very worthwhile thing in which to invest your time and money, especially if your profession centers on relationships with people (and really, all professions do).

How do you put yourself in the right places to meet excellent people? By taking advantage of good opportunities for quality networking, through both professional and personal associations. I stress quality networking, because it's actually more important to cultivate a few good sources than to spread yourself too thin. Networking expert Ivan Misner, founder of Business Networking International, and his co-authors of the book *Truth or Delusion: Busting Networking's Biggest Myths,* likens good networking to farming rather than hunting. It's more about careful cultivation over time. You can meet interesting people by taking courses on subjects you want to learn about and attending personal development and growth seminars that fire you up. You can meet people by participating in your favorite sport or hobby. You can meet people by attending social functions, alumni events, religious retreats, etc. They key is to put yourself out there in the kinds of places that attract other people who are building and/or living the kind of life that inspires you. Look around and be bold and courageous, even when considering circles where you want to be.

How do you recognize your ideal teammates?

To build a team of people who will inspire you, consider the very best, the Top 20%, of the people you know and admire, *including people who don't know you,* and create an ideal teammate profile, like the profiles introduced in Chapter 10. If you want different people on your team, for instance, a financial genius, a creative genius, and a supreme networker, then create a profile to be used as a filter when meeting people. Don't be too concerned about a perfect match: You also need to trust your instincts when you meet people who energize you and build relationships with those people with whom you share a strong chemistry and orientation for outstanding, balanced success.

## Building Strong Foundations

*"You can make more friends in two months by becoming interested in other people than you can in two years by trying to get other people interested in you."*
*- Dale Carnegie (1888-1955), personal development pioneer*


How do you usually make new friends or professional contacts? Do people introduce you to other people at parties and functions? What stops you from stepping up to someone you want to meet and introducing yourself? For many people, not knowing what to say in certain social situations or networking situations can be the biggest obstacle to success.

Being prepared will boost your confidence tremendously. Most (not all) conversations are simply a series of questions being asked and answered and stories being told. Therefore, in order to be confident in new situations where you want to establish new relationships, you need three things: questions, answers, and stories.

You need to have **questions** to ask and the true curiosity, interest, and ability to come up with new questions on the spot to deepen the conversation. *Practice* coming up with ice-breaker questions, rapport-building questions, and deeper, relationship-building inquiries. Use words like *who, what, where, when, how,* and *why* in your questions, rather than asking yes-or-no questions, in order to create a deeper dialog. If you make a list of 10 to 20 questions on paper, you'll not only have some good ones at the ready when you need them, you'll also improve your skill at coming up with good questions on the spot, so you can demonstrate how interested you are in others.

It is wise to be prepared with good **answers** to the questions that you may be asked. Obviously, you know where you live, but do you have something interesting to say about it? When people ask where I live, I don't just say, "Dobbs Ferry." I briefly embellish. "I live in Dobbs Ferry, one of the quaint, creative Hudson River villages north of Yonkers and Hastings-On-Hudson, and south of Irvington and Tarrytown's Tappan Zee Bridge." This gives the other person several cues and triggers to possibly relate to so that he or she is more likely to find something to say in response other than, "Oh."

When I'm asked what I do for a living, I also give more information than just my title. "I guide entrepreneurs and creative leaders in setting and achieving bold goals for a brighter future." *Practice* answering the questions you might be asked and come up with ways you can deepen a conversation by means of your thoughtful answers.

**Stories** that engage the listener inform, inspire, confirm credibility, and create shared experiences and bonding. The stories you tell can be your own most personal, vulnerable, or exciting experiences, as well as experiences and insights from other people's lives. The most engaging stories have some structure and flow: A good, brief story will convey a description of a situation, a challenge, or conflict that arose, the method of resolution employed (what happened), and resulting outcomes and feelings. *Practice* balancing brevity and humility with pride and confidence as you talk about something interesting that happened.

## Ice Breaker Questions

Here is a list of questions you can use to build new relationships. Ideally, you should write up some of your own and continually add new ones. Armed with these ice-breakers, you will be prepared to go out and meet and impress new people at all times.

- Where do you live? How do you get to and from work every day?
- What do you like most or least about your neighborhood?
- What kind of weather do you like most? What are your favorite outdoor sports or activities?
- The food is great here (or awful). What is your favorite meal of the day? If you could snap your fingers and food from anywhere in the world would instantly appear, what would your next meal be?
- Have you been traveling lately? What has been your favorite destination? What is your ideal fantasy vacation?
- Are you a collector? What do you collect? What is your latest exciting discovery?

123

- What is the best movie you've seen within the last year, and why?
- What subjects do you have your strongest opinions about?

You'll know you are on the right track when someone says, "Wow, that's a great question!" When you feel that there is a rapport building, you can lead into…

## Deeper Questions

You can ask these *heavier* questions once you have built an initial foundation for a rapport by listening and relating. In fact, if you want to have a conversation that will never be forgotten, try a few from this list and/or make up some questions from your own set of values and interests. Don't ask too many at once in a social setting. Do consider inviting someone to an extraordinary lunch, golf game, hike, or other focused setting in order to get to know each other even better:

- What gets you going in the morning? What motivates you most?
- What do you want your legacy to be?
- What is the most energizing aspect of your work?
- What is the most rewarding aspect of your work?
- What is the most draining aspect of your work?
- What is your most cherished childhood memory?
- What do people say are your greatest character traits? What do you like most about yourself?
- What pisses you off more than anything?
- What is missing from the area(s) of your life that are most meaningful to you? When do you plan to do something about that?
- What has been your most meaningful victory?
- What habits would you most like to give up, and what are you committed to changing this year?
- How would you describe your leadership style?
- What is the most thoughtful gift you ever got, gave, or saw someone get?

- What is the question you wish more people would ask you?
- Which of your goals are you most confident you'll achieve, and which ones do you have the most doubts about?
- If you were to throw the biggest celebration of your life one year from today, what accomplishments would you like to celebrate?

## Relevant Questions

So far, the questions we've listed (and the ones you've added to the list to inject your own voice) are useful in building strong relationships regardless of your purpose or specific line of business. The next collection of questions you need to prepare should be relevant to your goals and the goals of the person you are dealing with, thus leading to a sense of being on the same team. These are questions that can give you information and insight toward making requests – which leads more directly to having your income double with half the trouble.

- What's going on now that's GREAT?
- What's going on now that's not so great?
- What resources do you need to make it inevitable that you'll overcome your obstacles and reach your goals?
- What resources do most people turn to you for?
- How important is reaching your most important goal? What is it worth personally and financially?
- Who do you know who_____?
  (Fill in the blank with a request that would support your own goals! For example, "Who do you know at Madison Square Garden or a similar arena?"

The reason this approach to building relationships is so valuable is twofold. One reason is that people love to talk about themselves. Don't you love to talk about your interests, pursuits and passions? Don't you enjoy it when someone who also has an exciting life is listening to you tell your stories? Don't you enjoy hearing stories of extraordinary circumstances and inspiring victories? If you listen 80%

of the time and talk 20% of the time, you give your new friend a gift that is likely to be felt and appreciated on the deepest level.

The second reason is that you are gathering information about how to continue to build a relationship with the person. In the future, when you want to send the person a birthday card, interesting article, extraordinary photograph, or useful website link or otherwise feed the relationship with some thoughtful gesture, you'll know what is meaningful to the other person. Your questions help you find that out, and your stories trigger and inspire the other person to tell their stories, too.

If you invite people to discuss goals and challenges *big time,* you'll be more inspired and successful when playing your own big, extraordinary game! And you don't even have to ask them to be on your team: If they engage in the conversation, then they *are* on your team! All you have to do in order to manifest benefits from these relationships is to exchange requests.

## Making and Responding to Requests

I am a big believer in the motto "Givers gain," a business maxim that states that the more you share your good fortune, the more good fortune you attract! I encourage you to try and fulfill other people's requests in the right measure as compared with your own. If you've always been a people-pleaser, now is the time to include pleasing yourself and getting your own needs met as well as those of others. Use this chapter to create more requests for yourself. If you've been on the stingy, selfish side of the spectrum, use this chapter to create greater generosity, and then just watch and see how much you bring in via the law of attraction. But do it with no strings attached, or it will backfire.

For the purposes of this section on duplicating your Top 20%, we will focus on making bold requests of the people with whom you have already created strong relationships or with whom you are willing to try something different. By now, you've created profiles of your ideal client, your ideal mate, your ideal business partner, your ideal executive assistant, your ideal vacation plan, your ideal mortgage package, your ideal furniture set, or whatever you want to have "come-in" to your life. Now, it may just come to you by serendipity (I've seen that happen to a lot with people who get bold about clarifying their intentions and desires), but it is better to be proactive and not rely on coincidence. Don't expect it to fall in your lap out of nowhere. Now that you have a clear sense of what is ideal, you can ask for it! Every day, you have opportunities to make bold requests and have conversations that make a big difference.

Bold requests provide three significant benefits for you:

- By making bold requests for exactly what you want, you are more likely to get exactly what you want or at least something very close.
- By making bold requests, you build stronger bonds in relationships with people who are open to engaging in the best life has to offer.
- By making bold requests, you practice the art of finding the right approach, and you build confidence and skill, thereby making it more comfortable and less "bold" for you to ask for and get what you want in the future.

On the other hand, *not* making bold requests tends to hold you back in patterns that may not promote your growth and well-being over the long run:

- By not making bold requests, you leave everything to chance: Other people's needs and opinions may not leave you with much more than table scraps.
- By not making bold requests, you put up with people who put up with the status quo, surrounding yourself with followers instead of leaders. You also get known as a follower instead of a leader, which isn't as good for your income.
- By not making bold requests, you basically stay at the same level of skill, courage, and confidence, leaving you with less influence in changing your life for the better.

As an example, I made a bold request of a health coach I met a few years ago at a conference. I could tell from our initial conversations, which got pretty deep pretty quickly, that one of her biggest issues was a fear of commitment. I told her my observation and suggested that if she wanted to overcome it through coaching, we would have to extend the usual 90 day minimum commitment to a full year.

She was shocked that I made such an audacious suggestion, but we had built a good amount of rapport and were able to talk about it. She appreciated my "walking the talk" and understood how her commitment to our work would be the first in a series of beneficial decisions toward fulfilling her goals. She agreed to the program and had a very successful year. Several years later, I'm happy to report, she's leading health and wellness programs in the Virgin Islands (making profit and living the life!) and is happily married – two results that involved her own significant commitment as well as her newfound ability to engage commitment from others.

Another example of making bold requests comes from an entertainment attorney I worked with on expanding his professional network. Toward the end of a meeting with a contact, he used to simply say, "Let me know if there is anyone you think could use my services." This open-ended comment would lead to some referrals, but not enough to get by. He decided to get bolder and began asking specifically, "Who can you introduce me to?" This phrasing is a more direct request and call to action. Recently, he boldly asked this question of a very well-connected professional with whom he had recently gotten acquainted. "My new contact was surprised at first, but then got it and put me in touch with a friend at NBC and a few others."

If the idea of interacting with bigger players in the world scares you or makes you feel like procrastinating, then you'll need to either shift your frame of beliefs about what it means to relate with those people and/or muster up some courage to step out of your Comfort Zone. Through trial and error, and perhaps some coaching or training, you can begin to get comfortable with those people. You may need to learn and practice how to be attentive to other peoples' moods and navigate with great diplomacy. But don't let that stop you. Keep exploring various levels of rapport, and learn as much as you can about what will make the relationship extraordinary, no matter how long it takes.

I'd like to share with you two important questions to ask when moving projects forward, when making sales appointments, or when closing any kind of deal. The first is:

"What has to happen, on your side or for me to provide, for us to _____?" (Fill in the blank with what you want an outcome to be, an appointment, an introduction, or a sale).

The next question is:
"What else?"

If you use these questions to create and navigate a path to your ideal outcome, you'll know every step of the way what is necessary to move it to conclusion, or if the ideal outcome is not going to happen. If you are committed to achieve ideal outcomes with ideal people, you'll need this information and the rapport-building insights you gathered to create a road map for your persistence–one that balances generosity and self-interest.

Consider what I like to call "the S.W. Rule" as it applies to any request you make:

**Some Will, Some Won't, So What?**

Someone is Waiting to say yes to you!

---

### Challenge Homework

1. Make a list of who you'd want on your team.
2. Make your own list of questions that build rapport and another list for you to go deeper to create unforgettable conversations
3. Make a list of questions you "should" know the answer to and create a system to stay up to date on the answers.
4. Make a list of stories that you want to be clear and succinct in telling. Practice a few times so that you're fluid, but don't over-rehearse – you don't want to come across as "canned."
5. Make a list of people you have built relationships with and make a bold request or list of requests for the top five people on your list.
6. Identify a request you've made that you gave up on too easily, and find creative ways to revisit that request. Be persistent, but not a pain, and see how far you get. Remember, the results is a goal, but the relationship and your growth are more important than whether or not the person ultimately says yes or no.

# Chapter 13
## Systems, Structures and Time

*"Don't judge each day by the harvest you reap, but by the seeds you plant."*
*- Robert Louis Stevenson*

Now that you have ideas for clearing your path, attracting your ideal clients and providing great value and added value, you need to execute your plan. You need to take the steps, every day, every week, every month that will propel you forward— steps that involve networking, making calls, taking people to lunch, sending e-mails, researching, and much more. You will need a tremendous amount of self-discipline in order to go about implementing your plan and sticking with it, perhaps even after the initial excitement starts to wear off. However, if you have created a plan based on your ideal future and passion, it won't be any trouble at all.

If you are one of those people for whom setting and following a routine comes naturally, then you will have an easy time of it. However, if you find it difficult to stick to a daily regimen, especially if some of the actions you need to take are out of your comfort zone, then you may need to create new structures and systems for keeping focused on a winning game plan.

You know the difference between how you feel when you are on a regular exercise regime and when you are not? When you are consistent with your fitness program, it becomes virtually automatic to get to the gym, get onto your bike, go for a run or swim, play a few sets of tennis, or do whatever you do for exercise. It's easy to recognize that you enjoy the benefits daily, and staying healthy and strong becomes an integral part of your life. However, have you ever

131

stopped for three weeks or more and found it to be really hard to get started again? What if you stopped for three months? Isn't it like starting from scratch? It takes much more will power to start over again, so it is much better to make a habit and keep with it.

If you agree that building good habits is important, let's get at exactly what it takes to turn a hassle into a habit for the sake of your most meaningful goals. The answer is good systems and structures in your everyday life that reinforce constructive behaviors. Such structures and systems concern how you manage your time and energy. They are set up in such as way as to maintain regular, effortless, automatic, and successful habits. A few simple examples: your filing system is a structure for organizing your papers; your daily planner is a structure for managing your time; your bank account is a system for saving and managing your money; and any investment accounts you have are structures for increasing wealth. Your closets and dresser drawers are structures for organizing your wardrobe: they are systems you deal with when deciding how to present yourself to the world creating how you look every day. In fact, you could consider that everything you have had in your environment has been providing a systematic structure that supports exactly what you have attracted into your life up until now. If you want things to change, you must change the structures and systems in your environment.

Here's a simple example of how a structure can support the actions necessary for success. About twenty years ago, when I was in the recruiting business, my colleagues and I had tracking forms to write down the names of the people scheduled for interviews. **It was a simple tool, but was tied directly to our goals.** The more we filled up each tracking form with the names of people sent to qualified interviews, the more people got hired, and the more fees we earned. On any day of the week, simply by counting the number of interviews on my tracking form, I could see if I was on top of my game, or if I needed to step up my efforts. I always had my tracking form within reach on a clipboard so I could add to it or review it at any time.

## MEASURING SUCCESS

It is a widely recognized phenomenon, virtually a natural law, that whatever we measure and report, with the intention of improving, is much more likely to improve than if we don't measure or report our progress. Take Weight Watchers®, one of the most effective weight-loss programs in the world. There are a number of reasons that Weight Watchers® has been so successful, but the most important is reflected in the name of the organization: the watching, or tracking progress toward a goal, helps you reach that goal. The core Weight Watchers system is based on tracking points. You can eat whatever you want, as long as you don't exceed a certain number of points per week based on calories, fat content, and grams of fiber. If you exercise, you get extra credit points. Once a week, members go to meetings to weigh in, talk about their points chart, and listen to a speaker and other members who share inspiration, ideas, resources, and mutual encouragement. The effectiveness of the program comes from teaching new habits that are reinforced by using a very clear structure: using a scorecard of daily activities and food intake, and reporting results at weekly meetings.

When my wife was working the program, I got to see Weight Watchers® work its magic. An interesting pattern emerged, and as soon as she recognized it, she began to make steady progress that resulted in her losing over twenty-five pounds. She found that during the weeks that she used the daily tracking form, she always lost the two pounds per week that the program recommended as a healthy weight loss. If she got lazy, didn't want to do the math, or didn't count her points, she didn't lose the weight. The game was that simple: Don't count points, don't lose weight – or - count points, lose weight!

Weight Watchers® employs the physical and tangible act of reporting and tracking the actions that lead to successful accomplishment of a goal. That tracking creates a structure for consciousness and awareness of nutrition and portion choices that produces the desired results.

## The Daily Scorecard

Consider your pursuit a game that you're playing to win. View your goal like it's your own personal Super Bowl!

Basketball star Michael Jordan once said, "A coach will help you do what you don't want to do so you can be who you want to be." If you don't opt for a personal coach, the next best thing is a tool I call the Daily Scorecard. It is a self-coaching tool to support you until you learn and internalize new habits. It will help you cultivate and maintain a play-to-win attitude. You can create one of your own or download a Daily Scorecard that I made up by going to www.jf-executive-coaching.com/scorecard.xls.

The Daily Scorecard supports any goal that requires consistent daily and weekly actions. The point is to help you stay excited and engaged about tracking your goals and playing the game as a winner. If you are playing to win, you'll have more fun trying to score points, entering your points into your chart, rewarding yourself when you do well, learning and adjusting when you don't score as high as you'd like, and enjoying every moment along the way. Oh… and you're also more likely to win!

First, make the Daily Scorecard your own personal coaching system by filling in your name on the top line where it says "The Daily Scorecard for _____."

Column A lists the areas and actions that you want to track. I've put three popular section headings in that column, relating to three areas of business building: Current Clients, New Prospects, and Networking / Alliances. In each section, there are four blank lines, where you can put a word or phrase that describes the activity you want to track. For example, perhaps you want to make sure to do something extra for at least five clients per week. You could give yourself a point every time you do something special and unexpected for one of your current clients (a good way to provide added value and support an increase in your pricing later on!).

Under New Prospects, you can give yourself a point every time you reach someone new or send a proposal. Under Networking / Alliances, you can give yourself a point every time you attend a networking event or establish contact with someone influential who could send you more clients.

Feel free to write in any section heading and any actions that match your game plan, and set your points based on your goals.

In Column B, write the number of points for that action that represent your target: the ideal number of times you plan to take the action. Let's say that you wanted to do five "added value" actions for current clients per week. You would put a 5 in column B next to the line item "Client Extras." (See Figure 6).

| THE Daily SCORECARD for | Points | Week of | |
|---|---|---|---|
| © 2001 Jonathan Flaks Coaching Associates<br>www.jfcoach.com | | | M T W Th<br>F S S |
| .... | | | |
| CURRENT CLIENTS: | | | |
| Clients experiencing high level of re-<br>levant value | 10 | | |
| Do something unexpected to provide<br>added value | 5 | | |

**Figure 6** – The Daily Scorecard template

Once you have all your weekly and daily activities lined up and the scorecard lists how many points you are shooting for each week, you can start using it on a weekly basis. Keep a printout or an electronic file of your scorecard within arm's reach, and every day give yourself points for each successful activity you achieve. At the end of each week, count your points, and see how you did. Your first week's score is your baseline. There is no right or wrong number. What matters most, and what makes this tool work, is that you have a benchmark for yourself. And you'll know what your score will be when you have a "bull's-eye" week.

During each subsequent week, compare your score to your benchmark and other weeks. If you like percentages, either set up your scorecard initially to have all your points add up to 100, or each week simply do the math and divide your current score by the ideal score and find your percentage for that week. The goal is 100 percent, but the true purpose is to keep you aware of how you are doing each week and to measure what it truly does take to achieve your goal. It is important to use the Daily Scorecard to inspire you to make the adjustments necessary to increase your score week after week, until you're more naturally doing what it takes to succeed. In other words, play each week like a video game – shoot for beating your best score!

For example, if you find that you've only provided two clients any kind of extra attention in your first week, you know you have to be more attentive to this goal in your next weeks, until you are providing the excellence and added value you are committed to. With your scorecard, you'll be able to track how changes in your approach impact your results. You'll know what works and what doesn't as you steer your destiny to outstanding success!

For best results, report your results on a weekly basis to a coach, a buddy, or create an accountability group. If you make yourself accountable to someone who also wants to see you hit your goals, even your own, self-driven assignments, you'll have an added impetus to stay in action. You'll also have the additional benefit of thinking out loud with someone who will provide feedback, perspective, encouragement, and ideas, which is particularly useful if you fall behind and need to step up your efforts.

I'll give you another example of how this works. In 2005, my total cholesterol was 249, and in 2006 it went up to 267. It isn't healthy for anyone to be anywhere over 200 points combined HDL and LDL. I was aware that it was a problem, so I directed some attention on the matter, informally thinking about what I was eating and how often I was exercising. Bad news. By the end of 2007, my total cholesterol climbed to a dangerous high of 304! Just thinking about changing wasn't working. It was wake up time, so I committed myself to lowering my cholesterol to below 250 by March of 2008 and below 200 by June of 2008.

To reach that goal, I had to put a few practices on my daily scorecard:

| THE Daily SCORECARD for | Points | Week of --> | |
|---|---|---|---|
| © 2001 Jonathan Flaks Coaching Associates<br>www.jfcoach.com | | | M T W th<br>F S S |
| .... | | | |
| HEALTH AND VITALITY: | | | |
| Exercise 3-4 times per week | 4 | | |
| Drink at least 32 ounces of water daily | 7 | | |
| Take vitamin supplements at breakfast and dinner | 14 | | |
| Keep saturated fat intake below 10 g per day | 7 | | |
| Daily meditation and visualization | 7 | | |
| Check in with internist every 6 months for cholesterol blood work | | | |

**Figure 7** – My Daily Scorecard - Example

It wasn't easy for me to do everything right every week, but keeping score and knowing I would be "measuring in" with my doctor at specific intervals helped me stay aware and focused on what it would take to reach the goal. The results were thrilling: My cholesterol level dropped to 196 by January of 2008—six months earlier than I had hoped – without a pharmaceutical drug like Lipitor

Playing for your next high score may be its own reward. However, it may also be fun and add to your motivation if you set rewards for hitting certain milestones or for maintaining consistency in your daily and weekly routine. For best results, treat yourself to a reward that you wouldn't otherwise indulge in. Rewards can be simple and cost-efficient: some extra time alone or with a particular friend, a hike or a day sail, an extra set of tennis or nine holes of golf or half-day at the spa, perhaps a special meal. If the goal is big enough, consider a bigger reward, like a new big screen TV, a new car, jewelry, a SCUBA trip to the Caribbean, or whatever you would feel you deserve but might not splurge for without justification.

Other categories and ideas that you could use the Daily Scorecard for include:

### *Health and Vitality:*

- Go to gym 3 times per week
- Drink 8 glasses of water per day
- Stay on a reasonable diet plan every day or 6 days a week
- Drink 1 glass of wine (not more) per day
- Attend Weight Watchers® or other support group meeting weekly
- Stretch every night
- Floss every night

### *New Clients:*

- Number of networking events attended
- Number of new business cards distributed or received
- Number of interviews or appointments
- Number of proposals or the like

### *Relationships:*

- Make plans to see friends once per week (make the call by Thursday at noon)
- Respond to five e-mails on match.com (or other dating site or personal ads)
- Tell one friend per week about your ideal mate
- Schedule date night once per week with your spouse
- Tell your parents you love them once per month – in a different way each month
- Tell your children you love them once per week– in a different way each week

Similar itemized lists can be created for achieving a promotion and raise, reorganizing your personal finances or insurance needs, gaining proficiency in a new skill or talent such as learning a musical instrument, finding a new home, increasing sales, eliminating energy drains, improving your leadership and team-building capabilities, or anything else you are committed to having "come-in" to your life. You define the "income" that you're shooting for.

Here's another example of how the Daily Scorecard works and how it leads to new habits: When I started my coaching practice, I knew I had to be self-motivated in order to generate clients, and I found out early that this was not a service I could "sell." The only way people hired me was when I gave them a free sample session that truly addressed their concerns. However, I did have a strong commitment to building this profession quickly, and I subsequently found out that I was able to do so much more quickly than most people. Every day, my goal was to find people and offer them sample sessions. For every 10 sessions I completed, I'd start working with four new coaching clients. In any given month, two of those clients would discontinue, so to grow at the pace I wanted, I needed six new clients per month. Therefore, I had to schedule 15 sample sessions per month, or four per week. I used the Daily Scorecard to track and keep me focused on a few activities including networking, website development, speaking, and asking friends and clients for referrals. I maintained excellent momentum in generating a full client load in a very short number of months. After a while, the habits were automatic, and clients were coming in from referrals, so I no longer needed to use the Daily Scorecard.

In the construction industry, whenever concrete is poured, a frame of wood called a form guides the concrete to take the desired shape. Once the concrete is hardened, the form is removed. In the same way, you may find that the structures you put in place are necessary to support those habits that wouldn't otherwise take shape without help, but once they become habits or second nature, you won't need the tracking structure or scorecard anymore. By using the scorecard to build new habits, the goal is to have your habits occur without conscious effort or need for discipline—or, in other words, with half the trouble!

Remember to keep track of your "Tolerations" list, as we discussed in Chapter 5. If you outgrow any systems, replace or revise them. It is your responsibility to take care of the structures and systems in your environment. The more you take care of your environment and set it up to support your success, the more your environment will take care of you and support your success. Imagine and envision tracking systems and organizing structures that would ideally support your commitment, and then create those systems and structures in your physical space and see what happens.


## TIME

*Everything occurs in time.*

If you are like most of the professionals, consultants, and entrepreneurs that I meet, then keeping track of multiple priorities and making the best use of your time is a constant struggle. The best time management experts agree that you can't manage time—it's what you do with time that can be managed. Consider the quantity of time we measure as one minute. Sixty seconds. Think about a time you were engaged in a conversation catching up with an old friend, or talking through a challenging relationship issue, or doing a puzzle, or playing video games. Every minute, indeed every 30 minutes, seems to fly by. In contrast, recall how slowly time goes by when you're standing in front of the microwave oven waiting for your popcorn or soup to be cooked. Or how long a minute takes when you're waiting in the rain for the person who is late picking you up from the train station, or you're at the hospital waiting to hear the prognosis of a loved one.

Consider the Olympic speed skater who finds victory or defeat measured in hundredths of a second.

One minute can be an eternity. Try it right now. Just look at the clock as one minute goes by. Do nothing else. Just breathe and watch time slow down for one minute. If you are more conscious of time, you're less likely to go on auto-pilot and get sucked into time-wasting activities. If you live twice as present, it's like living twice as long because you're living twice as much life! Do you look at the clock when you're trying to get things done? Try it!

The most powerful concept in time-management theory is that of focus. Focus is the process of making clear decisions and choices. What will you pay attention to and for how long? That is the question you actually answer for yourself either consciously (on purpose) or automatically (unintentionally) thousands of time a day. How conscious and purposeful you are with this mental decision yields the level of focused productivity or scattered, wasted energy you experience in any given period of time. If you are deliberate about choosing where you put your attention, you are more likely to experience powerful results. If you practice being more conscious of each moment— keeping in mind at all times the idea that everything you do follows your conscious choices—you are going to recapture otherwise lost moments of time.

If you don't practice being more conscious and decisive, you leave the results to chance.

Focus is amplified by having a clear sense of commitment—a dedication and willingness to do whatever it takes to learn and grow as you shoot for a specific, meaningful goal. It's an attitude of playing a game to win, even if you might lose and learn, even if it's an area of your life that is very serious, like your health or your livelihood.

At any point in time, it is important to take a moment, especially if you find yourself off track, to ask yourself, "What am I committed to?" and "What's my best next step?" Then, your intuition can answer with the next doable action that moves you forward.


## Night-Before Planning

A superb strategy that is tremendously helpful on an ongoing basis is to *plan each day before it happens*. Each night, I look over my weekly goals derived from my annual and monthly strategic planning, and I look at my electronic calendar so I can see the time slots I have between appointments. Then I write my schedule on a blank page or dry-erase white board. For example, here is my plan for a typical day.

FRIDAY –

7:30 - Coaching Session - Peggy

8:30 - Breakfast and Family time

9:15 - Top Priority e-mails or quick calls

9:30 – Coaching Session - Dave

10:30 – *Work on Chapter 10*

11:30 – Return e-mails – schedule sessions for next week

12:00 – *Finish editing Chapter 10*

1:00 – Lunch

2:00 – Coaching Session - Leslie

3:00 – Confirm appointments / return e-mails and calls

3:30 – Organize material to delegate to Nancy (assistant) on

Monday

4:00 - Enjoy time with the kids.

We all know that planning your day gives you guidelines to help you stay focused on your highest priorities. However, if you've gotten out of the habit, I strongly recommend that you make a daily practice of planning your next day the night before it happens. Then you can start every day prepared to stay focused on your own "best bets" and not get thrown by distractions and interruptions that can start early and pull you off track. It isn't always possible to stick to your day plan perfectly, but as a guideline it will keep you as focused as possible.

If you find that any day doesn't go quite as planned, you can recreate a plan for the afternoon as soon as possible before you get too far off track.


## Mid-Day Re-Do

What happens if your plans get thrown by the circumstances in the day? As the old saying goes, "Man plans and God laughs!" If you create a well thought out day plan, you may still get distracted, overwhelmed, or simply interrupted by urgent matters or wonderful opportunities in the morning. How do you keep yourself from getting scattered in the afternoon?

In the seminars I lead on time management, I introduce a tool I call the Mid-Day Re-Do. The feedback I get from participants' surveys consistently point to it as a favorite. Quite simply, it is about giving yourself **permission** to repeat the day-mapping process even in the middle of the day. Using your night-before day-planning system, simply start from whatever time is current, and plan the remainder of your day. Let's say it's lunchtime, and your morning plan got thrown off course. Rather than feel like the day is a bust and letting yourself feel scattered and frustrated, simply ask yourself, "What is my BEST next step for 1:00... then what about 2:00...?" You can refocus on priorities that you didn't get to in the morning. You may find that you need to renegotiate some agreements if someone, including that eager part of yourself, is expecting a result from you at a particular time.

Following through with my example of a typical Friday, let's imagine that I didn't get a chance to finish editing Chapter 10 as I had hoped to complete from noon to 1:00 PM. My afternoon may be changed to look something like this:

FRIDAY –

1:00 – Lunch

2:00 – Coaching Session - Leslie

3:00 – Confirm appointments / return e-mails and calls

3:30 – Organize material to delegate to Nancy (assistant) on

Monday

4:00 - *Finish editing Chapter 10*

5:00 - Still have time to enjoy with the kids!

Having a sequence planned is better than not having a plan at all.

Another favorite quote from my time-management seminar is also surprisingly simple: "At the end of the day, you can only have done what you did!" Let's remember that it's not important to do *everything* on your to-do list all the time; life is too short to be that anal! Instead, focus on the top 20 percent of your choices that yield the best results, and some less important tasks may slip through unattended. Plan to use your time the best you can, and then accept the reality of each day and learn for the next one. If you make changes in how you work with time, you'll get more done this month than you did last month, and you'll be able to continue to build efficiency and effectiveness.

---

### Challenge Homework

1.  Set up your Daily Scorecard and have fun giving yourself points. Kick yourself into gear when you don't score as high as you'd like, and use it as a living, breathing tool to keep yourself excited about working on your game plan. Celebrate when you double your score compared with your baseline score.
2.  Practice planning your days the night before they start, and use the "Mid-Day Re-Do" on paper at least twice in the next week. Keep practicing until you get so good at time management that you are at least twice as effective with your time.

---

# Let's Go!

*"The secret to getting ahead is getting started. The secret to getting started is breaking your complex & overwhelming tasks into small manageable tasks, and then starting the first one."*
*– Mark Twain*

Now you see how the "Believe, Delete, and Duplicate" model can enable you to double your income with half the trouble. In the Believe section, you frame-shifted your fears, doubts, and concerns so you are now filled with energizing beliefs. You boosted your positive energy by having a strong commitment, a clear vision, and bold, exciting goals.

In the Delete section, you focused on eliminating energy drains and reducing your non-ideal involvements. You also learned how to deal with negative behavior in relationships. With new, higher standards, you have more time, energy and mental bandwidth for your very best resources.

In the Duplicate section, you focused on the choices that bring you 80% of your results and now you can identify and duplicate your "best bets." You explored brainstorming to multiply the value you provide to clients, and now have some new methods and time-management skills to implement your income doubling projects. Your discovery of how to enhance relationships and team-building are crucial to the whole process of leveraging. You now have all the tools you need and hopefully you've already begun to enjoy some significant gains.

Congratulations!

Thank you for your participation in this program – you did much more than read a book – you altered your life and I'll bet that you've already inspired many others around you. Always remember to be grateful for whatever good "comes-in" to your life. If you're twice as grateful, you can immediately feel a "double your income" kind of happiness!

Now imagine what your life would look like if you reviewed and leveraged these concepts and ideas and enjoyed having your income double with half the trouble, again! Take a look at the resources on the next few pages and perhaps review the Table of Contents to reinforce your learning. You'll know which concepts you need to spend more time on to understand more deeply, either by yourself or with some helpful coaching.

Keep believing in the brightest future possible for yourself and those you love. Continue deleting and deflecting energy drains and always shoot for the bulls-eye to duplicate and leverage your "best bets." I hope you enjoy every moment of every day!

# More Income~Doubling Resources from Jonathan Flaks Coaching

## DON'T GO IT ALONE

If you are serious about having your income double or even triple with half the trouble, you don't have to go at it alone, and you don't have to rely on your spouse or a friend to provide an intelligent ear to your concerns. Like I've done with the clients you've just read about, I can be the reliable, unbiased, business savvy, motivating person in your corner, without the cost, drama, profit sharing and potential legal headaches of an actual business partner. A free coaching session may be all you need to see if having your own personal coach would be right for you. The sample coaching session is the best value on the planet because YOUR ABILITY TO EARN MORE MONEY IS YOUR MOST LEVERAGABLE ASSET! There is no cost or obligation for the first session, but I only set aside a few time slots a month for sample coaching sessions. Grab your calendar and go to **www.freesamplesession.com** to sign up for one of my next available 30-minute time slots or call 877-700-BOLD (2653). You'll hang up the phone with new ideas, a focus for your next steps and the boost you need to move forward.

## Clearinghouse for more resources :

Bookmark **www.jfcoach.com** for up-to-date resources, programs, inspiring quotations and live events.

## More Inspiration:

Do you have a crystal clear, inspiring vision for your future? If not, you should! Having a clear vision statement keeps you productive and inspired every day because you'll be focused on the right goals and a meaningful purpose. A vision statement can be your foundation for testing big decisions and rallying people to your cause. And having passion for a vision can insure your happiness and health– far too many people get caught up in a stressful rat race to reach some financial success, only to find that they have no freedom or fulfillment. There is a better way.

**"Who Are You, Inc – Bringing Out Your Best In Business"** is a self-paced coaching program on CD that will guide you to having a powerful vision statement in writing. It's the perfect complement to this book. You'll have a clear, motivating "beacon" built on your own values. Many of my clients have told me that they have saved tons of money and years of unneeded therapy because they're excited to get out of bed every day. The CD is an exhilarating, eye opening experience that encompasses hundreds of dollars worth of coaching. Don't waste your life chasing the wrong rainbow. To read some testimonials and to grab your copy, go to **www.jfvisionquest.com**.

## "How to Stay On Track – Even On The Craziest Days"

This short free report provides a focused method for being more efficient and productive with your time, and what to do if you get off track. Plus, you'll get a tool for measuring the costs of your unproductive days and how to recoup those losses. With this information, you'll be better equipped to get more done and have more fun. Simply go to **www.yourproductivitypro.com** and follow the instructions for these free tips that are worth as much as you value your time.

## Live Appearances

To book Jonathan Flaks as a speaker for a **customized** motivational keynote address, workshop, training seminar, teleconference, or lunch-n-learn program, **call 877-700-BOLD (2653)**

Jonathan's live programs are not canned presentations – they're structured as dynamic **"live coaching" sessions,** guaranteed to fully engage every audience member in deeper learning and goal setting. With his upbeat, conversational style, interactive exercises, real world examples, and thought-provoking stories, Jonathan's most popular topics have been:

➢ **"Inspiring Confidence in Challenging Times"**

Ideas to maintain your own motivation and be a positive influence.

➢ **"Income Double / Half the Trouble"**

You CAN earn more money, more easily, doing what you love to do.

➢ **"Get Up – Stay Up"**

Seven secrets for getting and STAYING energized.

➢ **"Small Business Team Dynamics"**

Unique leadership skills for entrepreneurs and consulting firms.

## About the Author

**Jonathan Flaks, M.C.C.** is an internationally recognized Business Success and Team Leadership Coach. Since 1998, he has guided hundreds of entrepreneurs, executives, consultants and professionals to achieve consistent motivation, focus, and bold accomplishments. Many clients have doubled their income with half the trouble. Clients have come from Morgan Stanley, BMG Entertainment, KPMG, IBM, Disney, Deloitte, Honeywell, Goldman Sachs, and other entrepreneurial and professional service firms.

Jonathan draws from a diverse, 20-year business communication and consulting background. He is founder and lead facilitator for Infinite Achievement Circles (IAC), founder of the Westchester, New York, chapter of the International Coach Federation (ICF), and has spearheaded fundraising events for the Make-A-Wish Foundation.

Jonathan maintains "Master Certified Coach" credentials from the International Coach Federation. He completed a dual degree from Cornell University and was Adjunct Professor of Business Leadership and Coaching Skills at New York University. In addition to this book, Jonathan created *"Who Are You, Inc., - Bring Out Your Best In Business,"* an audio program that empowers professionals to create vision statements.

He lives in Dobbs Ferry, New York.

## A Personal Note from the Author:

In addition to experience and credentials, character and personal chemistry are always important in relationships. Here are a few things you may not see in a traditional bio. I'll try to be humble, but I'm told to toot my own horn here!

My personal passions include:

- My wife, Ellen, and our two rockin' sons
- All classic rock music: my favorite groups are Yes, Led Zeppelin, The Who, Pink Floyd, The Beatles, The Grateful Dead, The Doors, and Van Morrison.
- Playing piano and singing, performing solo and with my band.
- Being on or in the water: sailing, SCUBA , swimming
- Tennis, biking and skiing
- Favorite foods lobster, chocolate pudding pie, a nice crisp apple

I'm told that enthusiasm, creativity, boldness, honesty, and business savvy are my strongest character traits. I'm passionate about helping people leverage their natural talents, hidden strengths, and untapped resources to make twice the money with half the stress. I've done it myself twice – it's an amazing conversation. I love what I do, I do what I love, and life is an extraordinary adventure.

I care deeply about my clients, and I practice getting to the heart of the matter quickly. I believe all people are infinitely creative and resourceful and working together people can navigate the obstacles much faster and easier.

Please contact me at **jonathan@jfcoach.com** or 877-700-BOLD(2653) to talk about your passions and how to enjoy more of them in your life.

877-700-BOLD (2653)
*www.jfcoach.com*
*jonathan@jfcoach.com*

Breinigsville, PA USA
19 January 2011
253390BV00008B/2/P